ZHUANGZI SPEAKS

ZHUANGZI SPEAKS

The Music of Nature

ADAPTED AND ILLUSTRATED BY

TSAI CHIH CHUNG

TRANSLATED BY

Brian Bruya

AFTERWORD BY DONALD J. MUNRO

LETTERED BY WAYNE TRUMAN

PRINCETON UNIVERSITY PRESS

PRINCETON, NEW JERSEY

Copyright © 1992 by Princeton University Press
Published by Princeton University Press, 41 William Street,
Princeton, New Jersey 08540
In the United Kingdom: Princeton University Press, Chichester,
West Sussex

Library of Congress Cataloging-in-Publication Data

Tsai Chih Chung, 1948–
[Tzu jan te hsiao sheng. English]
Zhuangzi speaks: the music of nature / adapted and illustrated by
Tsai Chih Chung; translated by Brian Bruya; afterword by
Donald J. Munro
p. cm.
Translation of: Tzu jan te hsiao sheng.
ISBN 0-691-00882-5 (alk. paper : pbk.)
ISBN 0-691-05694-3 (cl.)
1. Chuang-tzu. Nan-hua ching. 2. Tao. I. Chuang-tzu.
II. Bruya, Brian, 1966– . III. Title.
BL1900.C576T73 1992
299′.51482—dc20 92-6754

Princeton University Press books are printed on acid-free paper
and meet the guidelines for permanence and durability of the
Committee on Production Guidelines for Book Longevity of
the Council on Library Resources

Printed in the United States of America
11 13 15 17 16 14 12

ISBN-13: 978-0-691-00882-0 (pbk.)

CONTENTS

vii   *Acknowledgments*

ix   *Guide to Pronunciation*

xiii   *Map*

5   The Summer Cicada and the Wonder Tortoise

7   The Little Sparrow's Small Happiness

8   Hui Shi's Giant Gourd

10   The Song Family's Secret Formula

12   The Useless *Shu* Tree

15   The Tattooed Yue People

16   The Music of the Earth

19   Zhao Wen Quits the Zither

20   Does Wang Ni Know?

22   Is Xi Shi Really Beautiful?

23   Li Ji's Tears

24   Zhang Wuzi's Dream

25   Shadows Talking

26   The Dream of the Butterfly

27   Three at Dawn and Four at Dusk

28   Hui Shi Leans against a Tree

29   The Cook Carves Up a Cow

31   Passing on the Flame

32   The Caged Pheasant

33   Like A Mantis Stopping a Cart

35   The Horse Lover

36   The Earth Spirit's Tree

38   A Tree's Natural Life Span

40   The Freak

41   Oil Burns Itself Out

42   The Tiger Trainer

43   Toeless Shu

44   Nature the Superhero

45   Forgetting the Dao

46   Zi Sang Questions His Fate

47   Digging a Canal in the Ocean Floor

48   Are a Duck's Legs Too Short?

49   The Lost Goat

50   Bandits Have Principles, Too

52   Good Wine, Bad Wine

CONTENTS

53 The Yellow Emperor Questions Guangcheng

54 Nature's Friend

55 The Old Wheelwright

57 The Earth and the Sky

58 Crows and Seagulls

59 Confucius Sees a Dragon

60 Don't Ring the Bull's Nose

61 The Wind and the Snake

63 Courage of the Sage

65 The Frog in the Well

68 Learning How to Walk in Handan

69 A Crow Eating a Dead Rat

71 You're Not a Fish

72 Zhuangzi Dreams of a Skeleton

74 Sea Birds Don't Like Music

76 The Drunk Passenger

77 Riding with the Dao

79 The Sweet Water is Gone First

81 Lin Hui Forsakes a Fortune

82 Swallows Nest in the Eaves

83 The Mantis Getting the Cicada

85 Fan Was Never Destroyed

86 Knowledge and the Dao

88 Gengsang Forsakes Fame

89 The Yellow Emperor and the Pasture Boy

91 The Stone Mason and the Ying Man

93 Two Nations on a Snail's Antennae

94 Zhuangzi Borrows Grain

95 The Turtle That Could Predict the Future

97 Natural Use

98 Catch the Fish, Discard the Trap

99 Yang Zhu Studies the Dao

100 Zi Gong's Snow-White Clothes

102 The Bandit Speaks

107 Zhuangzi's Three Swords

114 Confucius in the Black Forest

117 The Man Who Hated His Footprints

118 The Man Who Hated His Shadow

119 Like a Drifting Boat

120 The Dragonslayer

122 Shattering the Dragonpearl

124 Don't Make Sacrifices

125 Zhuangzi on His Deathbed

127 *Afterword, by Donald J. Munro*

ACKNOWLEDGMENTS

I owe a great many thanks to all my friends, colleagues, and teachers in Taiwan for my progress in the Chinese language. I also owe much to Professor Huang Chun-chieh for teaching me the fundamentals of Chinese thought. In addition, I am very grateful to Professor Donald Munro for writing the afterword and to Lian Xinda for proofreading and suggesting many useful corrections.

More thanks than I can possibly express here go to Tsai Chih Chung, who exemplifies the Dao in every way and was gracious enough to share his understanding with us through his ingenious artwork.

Brian Bruya

GUIDE TO PRONUNCIATION

There are different systems of Romanization of Chinese words, but in all of these systems the sounds of the letters used do not necessarily correspond to those sounds which we are accustomed to using in English (for instance, would you have guessed that *zh* is pronounced like *j*?). Of course these systems can be learned, but to save some time and effort for the reader who is not a student of Chinese, we have provided the following pronunciation guide. The Chinese words appear on the left as they do in the text and are followed by their pronunciations. Just sound out the pronunciations and you will be quite close to the proper Mandarin Chinese pronunciation.

notes:

-dz is a combination of *d* and *z* in one sound, without the *ee* sound at the end; so it sounds kind of like the sound of a bee in flight with a slight *d* sound at the beginning.

-ts is mostly the *ss* sound with a slight *t* (minus the *ee*) sound at the beginning.

-ew is pronounced like the *ew* in f*ew*.

-ow is pronounced like the *ow* in n*ow*.

-aw is pronounced like the *aw* in th*aw*.

Ba: baw
Beijing: bay-jeeng
Bian: byen
Bohai: bwo-high

Cai: tsigh (rhymes with high)
Chen: chun
Chu: choo

Da Wei: daw way
Dao: dow
Daodejia: dow-du (*u* as in p*u*ll)-jyaw
Daojia: dow-jyaw
De: du (*u* as in p*u*ll)

Fan: fawn
Fu: foo

Gengsang: gung-sawng
Guangcheng: gwawng-chung

Han: hawn
Handan: hawn-dawn
Huan: hwawn
Huang Chun-chieh: hwawng jwun-jye

Huang-Lao: hwawng-low (rhymes with now)
Hui Shi: hway sure
Huizi: hway-dz

Ji: jee
Jia: jyaw
Jian He: jyen-hu (*u* as in p*u*ll)
Jian Wu: jyen oo
Jin: jeen
Juci: jew-ts
Ju Que: jew chweh

Kongzi: kong (long o)-dz
Kuang Jieyu: kwawng jyeh-yew
Kuei: Kway

Lai: lie
Laozi: low (rhymes with now)-dz
Li: lee
Li Ji: lee jee
Liang: lyawng
Lin Hui: leen hway
Liu Xiaogan: lyo (long o) shyow-gone
Liuxia Ji: lyoh-shyaw jee
Lu: loo

Man: mawn
Mengzi: mung-dz
Mozi: mwo-dz

Nanguoziqi: nawn-gwo-dz-chee
Nie Que: nyeh chweh

Peng: pung
Peng Zu: pung dzoo

Qi: chee
Qin: cheen

Qu Boyu: chyew bwo-yew

Ri Zhongshi: rr jong (long o)-sure

Shang: Shawng
Shang Yang: shawng yawng
Shicheng: sure chung
Shu: shoo
Shu Shan: shoo shawn
Shun: shwoon (*oo* as in b*oo*k)
Sima Tan: sz-maw tawn
Song: song (long o)
Su Qin: soo cheen

Tai: tie
Tang: tawng
Tsai Chih Chung: tsigh (rhymes with high) jir jong (long o)

Wang Liang: wawng lyawng
Wang Ni: wawng nee
Wei: way
Wei Lei: way lay
Wu: oo
Wu-wei: oo-way
Wu Qi: oo chee

Xi Shi: shee sure
Xian: shyen
Xunzi: shwun-dz

Yan: yen
Yan He: yen hu (*u* as in p*u*ll)
Yan Hui: yen hway
Yang: yawng
Yang Hu: yawng hoo
Yang Zhu: yawng joo
Yangtze: yawng-dz

Yao: yow

Yin: een

Ying: eeng

Yu Ju: ew jew

Yuan Xian: ywen shyen

Yuanju: ywen-jew

Yue: yweh

Zang: dzawng

Zhang Wuzi: jawng oo-dz

Zhang Yi: jawng ee

Zhao: jow

Zhao Wen: jow wun

Zheng: jung

Zhi: jir

Zhi Lishu: jir lee-shoo

Zhili Yi: jir-lee ee

Zhong You: jong (long o) yo

Zhongshan: jong (long o)-shawn

Zhou: joe

Zhuang Zhou: jwawng joe

Zhuangzi: jwawng-dz

Zhuping Man: joo-peeng mawn

Zi: dz

Zi Gong: dz gong (long o)

Zi Sang: dz sawng

Zi Yu: dz yew

Ziyou: dz-yo

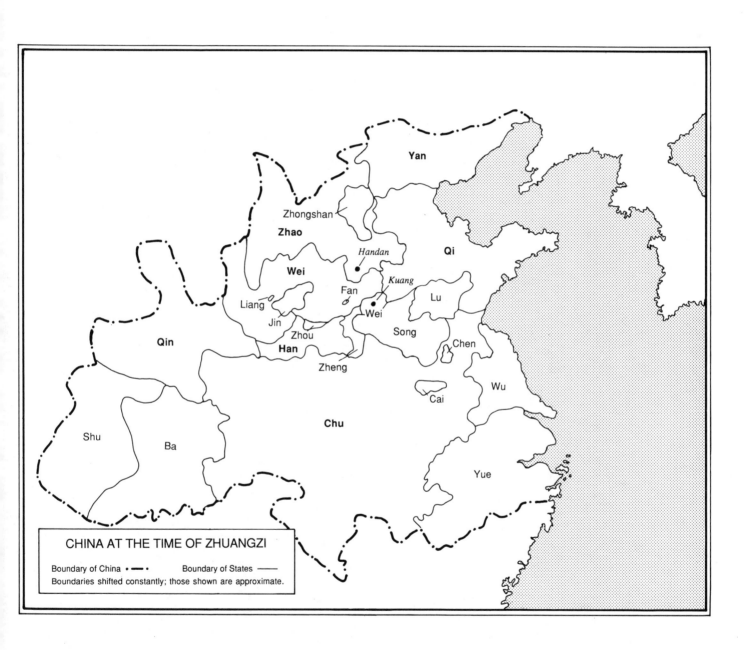

CHINA AT THE TIME OF ZHUANGZI

Boundary of China ·—·—·   Boundary of States ——

Boundaries shifted constantly; those shown are approximate.

ZHUANGZI SPEAKS

The Music of Nature

莊子者，蒙人也，名周。周嘗為蒙漆園吏，與梁惠王、齊宣王同時。其學無所不闚，然其要本歸於老子之言。故其著書十餘萬言，大抵率寓言也。作漁父、盜跖、胠篋，以詆訿孔子之徒，以明老子之術。畏累虛、亢桑子之屬，皆空語無事實。然善屬書離辭，指事情類，用剽剝儒墨，雖當世宿學不能自解免也。其言洸洋自恣以適己，故自王公大人不能器之。

節自〔漢・司馬遷◎史記〕

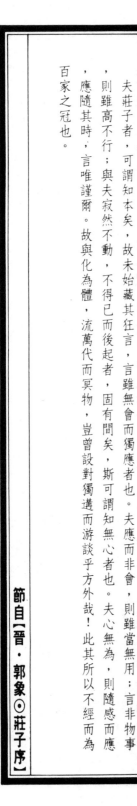

夫莊子者，可謂知本矣，故未始藏其狂言，言雖無會而獨應者也。夫應而非會，則雖當無用；言非物事，則雖高不行；與夫寂然不動，不得已而後起者，固有間矣，斯可謂知無心者也。夫心無為，則隨感而應，應隨其時；言唯謹爾。故與化為體，流萬代而冥物，豈曾設對獨遘而游談乎方外哉！此其所以不經而為百家之冠也。

節自【晉・郭象◎莊子序】

THE NAME OF OUR HERO IS ZHUANG ZHOU. LIKE ALL CHINESE NAMES, THE SURNAME COMES FIRST, FOLLOWED BY THE GIVEN NAME. TO SHOW RESPECT FOR HIS VAST WISDOM, WE ADD THE SUFFIX "ZI" TO HIS SURNAME, JUST LIKE KONGZI (CONFUCIUS), MENGZI (MENCIUS), AND LAOZI. ZHUANGZI LIVED DURING THE FOURTH CENTURY B.C., A TIME KNOWN AS THE WARRING STATES PERIOD IN CHINA. THIS WAS A PERIOD OF DISUNITY IN WHICH RIVAL NATIONS BATTLED CONSTANTLY FOR MORE LAND AND GREATER POWER. AS A RESULT, IT WAS ALSO A TIME OF WIDESPREAD DEATH AND DESTRUCTION. ZHUANGZI SAW THIS CHAOS AND SUFFERING AND WAS DEEPLY SADDENED BY IT.

AS A WAY OUT, ZHUANGZI SHIFTED HIS LINE OF SIGHT FROM THE EARTHLY WORLD TO THE LIMITLESSNESS OF TIME AND SPACE.

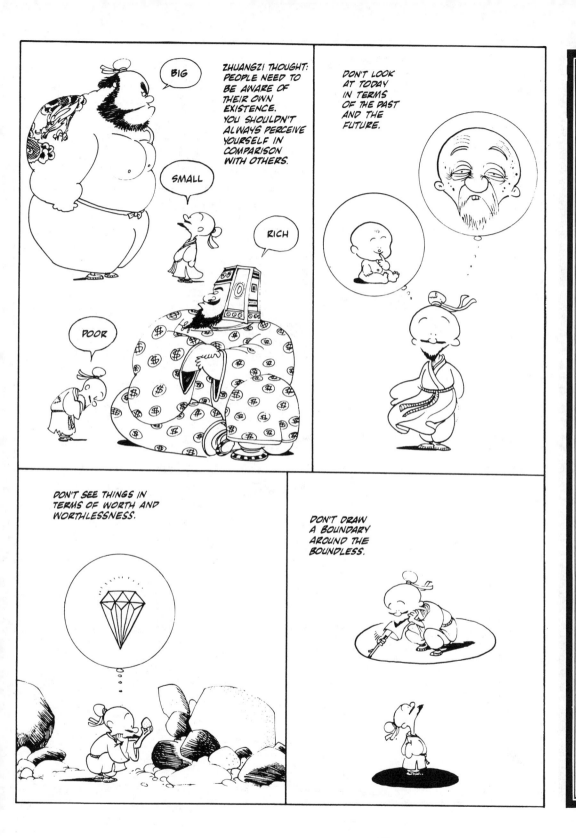

莊子者，姓莊，名周，（太史公云：字子休。）梁國蒙縣人也。六國時，為漆園吏，與魏惠王、齊宣王、楚威王同時，（李頤云：與齊愍王同時。）齊楚嘗聘以為相，不應。時人皆尚遊說，莊子獨高尚其事，優遊自得，依老氏之旨，著書十餘萬言，以消遙自然無為齊物而已；大抵皆寓言，歸之於理，不可案文責也。

節自【唐・陸德明◉莊子序】

3

DON'T DRAW LIFE FROM DEATH. ONLY IN THIS WAY CAN YOU ATTAIN LIMITLESS FREEDOM.

THE PHILOSOPHY OF ZHUANGZI IS A PHILOSOPHY OF FREEDOM. IT IS A PHILOSOPHY THAT TAKES LIFE AND HURLS IT INTO THE LIMITLESSNESS OF TIME AND SPACE IN ORDER TO BE EXPERIENCED TO THE FULLEST.

TO ZHUANGZI, THE WORLD WAS CHAINED BY A "LIFELESS ORDER," SO WHAT HE PURSUED INSTEAD WAS A "LIVELY DISORDER."

夫莊子者，所以申道德之深根，述重玄之妙旨，暢无為之恬淡，明獨化之窅冥，鉗揵九流，括囊百氏，諒區中之至教，實象外之微言者也。

其人姓莊，名周，字子休，生宋國睢陽蒙縣，師長桑公子，受號南華仙人。當戰國之初，降周之末，歎蒼生之業薄，傷道德之陵夷，乃慷慨發憤，爰著斯論。其言大而博，其旨深而遠，非下士之所聞，豈淺識之能究！

節自【唐‧成玄英◎莊子序】

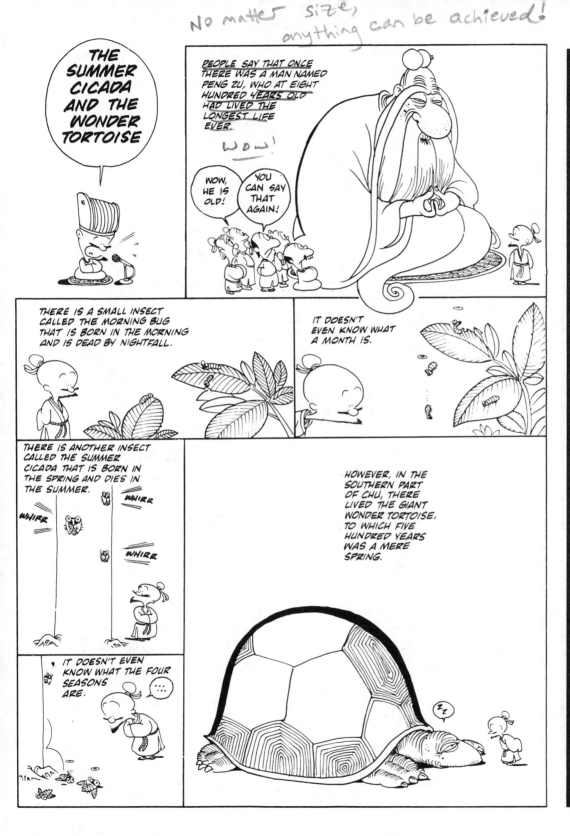

【莊子◉逍遙遊第一】

小知不及大知，小年不及大年。奚以知其然也？朝菌不知晦朔，蟪蛄不知春秋，此小年也。楚之南有冥靈者，以五百歲為春，五百歲為秋；上古有大椿者，以八千歲為春，八千歲為秋。而彭祖乃今以久特聞，眾人匹之，不亦悲乎！

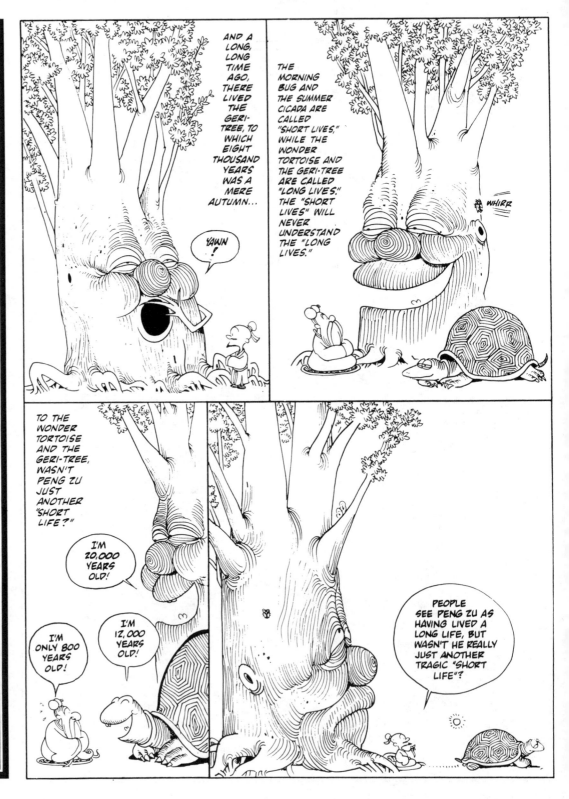

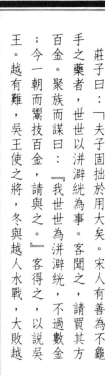

莊子曰：「夫子固拙於用大矣。宋人有善為不龜手之藥者，世世以洴澼絖為事。客聞之，請買其方百金。聚族而謀曰：『我世世為洴澼絖，不過數金；今一朝而鬻技百金，請與之。』客得之，以說吳王。越有難，吳王使之將，冬與越人水戰，大敗越人，裂地而封之。能不龜手，一也；或以封，或不免於洴澼絖，則所用之異也。今子有五石之瓠，何不慮以為大樽而浮乎江湖，而憂其瓠落無所容？則夫子猶有蓬之心也夫！」

【莊子◎逍遙遊第一】

宋人有善為不龜手之藥者，世世以洴澼絖為事。

客聞之，請買其方百金。聚族而謀曰：『我世世為洴澼絖，不過數金；今一朝而鬻技百金，請與之。』

客得之，以說吳王。越有難，吳王使之將，冬與越人水戰，大敗越人，裂地而封之。能不龜手，一也；或以封，或不免於洴澼絖，則所用之異也。

AT THAT TIME, THE STATES OF WU AND YUE WERE BITTER ENEMIES.

AFTER GETTING THE SECRET FORMULA FOR THIS MEDICINE, THE KING OF WU LAUNCHED A WINTER OFFENSIVE ON WATER.

THE WU ARMY RELIED ON THIS MEDICINE NOT TO GET FROSTBITE, BUT THE YUE SOLDIERS WERE UNPROTECTED. AS A RESULT, THE YUE ARMY WAS TERRIBLY DEFEATED.

AFTER THE DEFEAT OF THE YUE KINGDOM, THE TRAVELER WHO PRESENTED THE SECRET FORMULA TO THE KING OF WU WAS PRESENTED WITH A LARGE ESTATE AND LIVED THE LIFE OF A NOBLEMAN THEREAFTER.

ALTHOUGH IT WAS THE SAME FORMULA, SOME PEOPLE DIDN'T KNOW HOW TO USE IT, SO THEY SPENT THEIR LIVES BLEACHING CLOTH. BUT WHEN A FLEXIBLE PERSON WHO COULD THINK OF NEW IDEAS CAME ALONG, HE ENDED UP LIVING THE LIFE OF A WEALTHY MAN.

宋人有善為不龜手之藥者，世世以洴澼絖為事。客聞之，請買其方百金。聚族而謀曰：『我世世為洴澼絖，不過數金；今一朝而鬻技百金，請與之。』客得之，以說吳王。越有難，吳王使之將，冬與越人水戰，大敗越人，列地而封之。能不龜手，一也；或以封，或不免於洴澼絖，則所用之異也。

【莊子●逍遙遊第一】

11

THE USELESS SHU TREE

【莊子⊙逍遙遊第一】

惠子謂莊子曰：「吾有大樹，人謂之樗。其大本擁腫而不中繩墨，其小枝卷曲而不中規矩，立之塗，匠者不顧。今子之言，大而無用，眾所同去也。」

莊子曰：「子獨不見狸狌乎？卑身而伏，以候敖者；東西跳梁，不辟高下；中於機辟，死於罔罟。

今夫斄牛，其大若垂天之雲。此能為大矣，而不能執鼠。今子有大樹，患其無用，何不樹之於無何有之鄉，廣莫之野，彷徨乎無為其側，逍遙乎寢臥其下。不夭斤斧，物無害者，無所可用，安所困苦哉！」

Nothing goes to waste in nature?

HUIZI ONCE SAID TO ZHUANGZI:

I HAVE THIS GIANT TREE CALLED A SHU TREE. ITS TRUNK IS ALL LUMPS AND BUMPS AND WINDS THIS WAY AND THAT.

Lumps & Bumps

ITS BRANCHES ARE ALL GNARLED AND TWISTED. A CARPENTER'S PLUMB LINE COULD NEVER BE USED ON IT.

IT GROWS RIGHT BESIDE THE ROAD, AND NO CARPENTER HAS EVER PAID ANY ATTENTION TO IT.

Rlly?

THE WORDS YOU HAVE BEEN SPEAKING LATELY ARE JUST LIKE THIS TREE, BIG AND USELESS. WHO'S GOING TO LISTEN TO YOU?

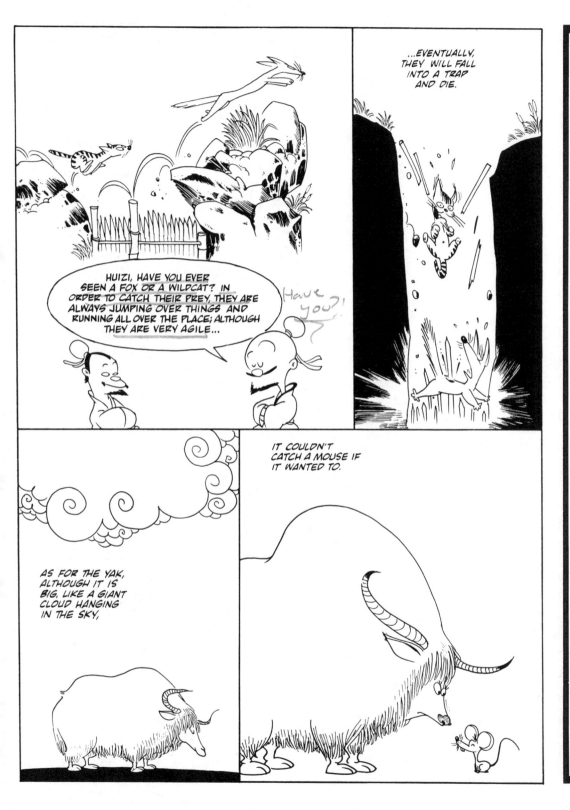

惠子謂莊子曰：「吾有大樹，人謂之樗。其大本擁腫而不中繩墨，其小枝卷曲而不中規矩，立之塗，匠者不顧。今子之言，大而無用，眾所同去也。」

莊子曰：「子獨不見狸狌乎？卑身而伏，以候敖者；東西跳梁，不辟高下；中於機辟，死於罔罟。今夫斄牛，其大若垂天之雲。此能為大矣，而不能執鼠。今子有大樹，患其無用，何不樹之於無何有之鄉，廣莫之野，彷徨乎無為其側，逍遙乎寢臥其下。不夭斤斧，物無害者，無所可用，安所困苦哉！」

【莊子◉逍遙遊第一】

惠子謂莊子曰：「吾有大樹，人謂之樗。其大本擁腫而不中繩墨，其小枝卷曲而不中規矩，立之塗，匠者不顧。今子之言，大而無用，眾所同去也。」

莊子曰：「子獨不見狸狌乎？卑身而伏，以候敖者；東西跳梁，不辟高下；中於機辟，死於罔罟。

今夫斄牛，其大若垂天之雲。此能為大矣，而不能執鼠。今子有大樹，患其無用，何不樹之於無何有之鄉，廣莫之野，彷徨乎無為其側，逍遙乎寢臥其下。不夭斤斧，物無害者，无所可用，安所困苦哉！」

【莊子◎逍遙遊第一】

14

我，汝知之乎？女聞人籟而未聞地籟，女聞地籟而未聞天籟夫！

子游曰：「敢問其方。」

子綦曰：「夫大塊噫氣，其名為風。是唯无作，作則萬竅怒呺。而獨不聞之翏翏乎？山林之畏佳，

17

大木百圍之竅穴，似鼻似口，似耳，似枅，似圈，似臼，似洼者，似污者；激者，謞者，叱者，吸者，叫者，譹者，宎者，咬者，前者唱于而隨者唱喁。冷風則小和飄風則大和，厲風濟則眾竅為虛。而獨不見之調調，之刁刁乎？」

【莊子◎齊物論第二】

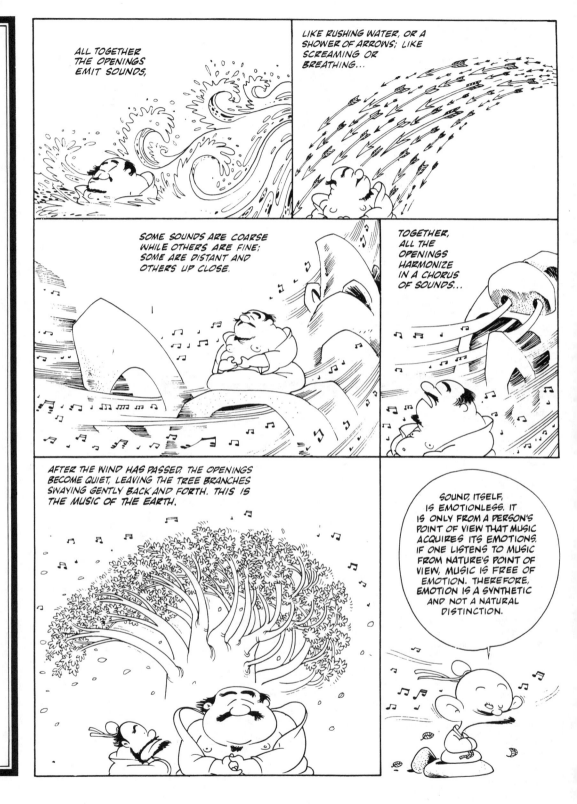

18

古之人，其知有所至矣。惡乎至？有以為未始有物者，至矣，盡矣，不可以加矣。其次以為有物矣，而未始有封也。其次以為有封焉，而未始有是非也。是非之彰也，道之所以虧也。道之所以虧，愛之所以成。果且有成與虧乎哉？果且无成與虧乎哉？有成與虧，故昭氏之鼓琴也；無成與虧，故昭氏之不鼓琴也。

【莊子◉齊物論第二】

19

齧缺問乎王倪曰：「子知物之所同是乎？」

曰：「吾惡乎知之！」

「子知子之所不知邪？」

曰：「吾惡乎知之！」

「然則物无知邪？」

曰：「吾惡乎知之！雖然，嘗試言之。庸詎知吾所謂知之非不知邪？庸詎知吾所謂不知之非知邪？且吾嘗試問乎女：民溼寢則腰疾偏死，鰌然乎哉？木處則惴慄恂懼，猨猴然乎哉？三者孰知正處？

民食芻豢，麋鹿食薦，蝍蛆甘帶，鴟鴉耆鼠，四者孰知正味？猨猵狙以為雌，麋與鹿交，鰌與魚游。毛嬙麗姬，人之所美也；魚見之深入，鳥見之高飛，麋鹿見之決驟。四者孰知天下之正色哉？自我觀之，仁義之端，是非之塗，樊然殽亂，吾惡能知其辯！

【莊子⊙齊物論第二】

21

且吾嘗試問乎女：民濕寢則腰疾偏死，鰍然乎哉？木處則惴慄恂懼，猨猴然乎哉？三者孰知正處？民食芻豢，麋鹿食薦，蝍蛆甘帶，鴟鴉耆鼠，四者孰知正味？猨猵狙以為雌，麋與鹿交，鰍與魚游，毛嬙麗姬，人之所美也；魚見之深入，鳥見之高飛，麋鹿見之決驟。四者孰知天下之正色哉？自我觀之，仁義之端，是非之塗，樊然殽亂，吾惡能知其辯！

【莊子◎齊物論第二】

LI JI'S TEARS

ON LI JI'S WEDDING DAY, SHE WAS TO BE MARRIED AGAINST HER WILL TO PRINCE XIAN OF JIN. SHE WAS SO SAD THAT SHE DRENCHED HER WEDDING DRESS IN TEARS.

I'M NOT MARRYING HIM! I WON'T DO IT!

BUT AFTER SHE WAS MARRIED, SHE FOUND HERSELF SLEEPING ON A LONG, SOFT BED AND EATING FOOD FROM THE FOUR CORNERS OF THE EARTH. WHO WOULD BELIEVE THAT ON HER WEDDING DAY SHE CRIED HER EYES OUT?

EVERYONE IS AFRAID OF DYING, BUT MAYBE DEATH WILL BE SO GREAT THAT WE'LL END UP REGRETTING HAVING EVER LIVED.

予嘗為女妄言之，女以妄聽之。奚旁日月，挾宇宙？為其脗合，置其滑涽，以隷相尊。衆人役役，聖人愚芚，參萬歲而一成純。萬物盡然，而以是相蘊。

予惡乎知說生之非惑邪！予惡乎知惡死之非弱喪而不知歸者邪！麗之姬，艾封人之子也。晉國之始得之也，涕泣沾襟；及其至於王所，與王同筐牀，食芻豢，而後悔其泣也。予惡乎知夫死者不悔其始之蘄生乎！

【莊子◎齊物論第二】

23

夢飲酒者，旦而哭泣；夢哭泣者，旦而田獵。方其夢也，不知其夢也。夢之中又占其夢焉，覺而後知其夢也。且有大覺而後知此其大夢也，而愚者自以為覺，竊竊然知之。君乎，牧乎，固哉！丘也與女，皆夢也；予謂女夢，亦夢也。是其言也，其名為弔詭。萬世之後而一遇大聖，知其解者，是旦暮遇之也。

【莊子◉齊物論第二】

〔莊子◎齊物論第二〕

昔者莊周夢為胡蝶，栩栩然胡蝶也，自喻適志與！不知周也。俄然覺，則蘧蘧然周也。不知周之夢為胡蝶，胡蝶之夢為周與？周與胡蝶，則必有分矣。此之謂物化。

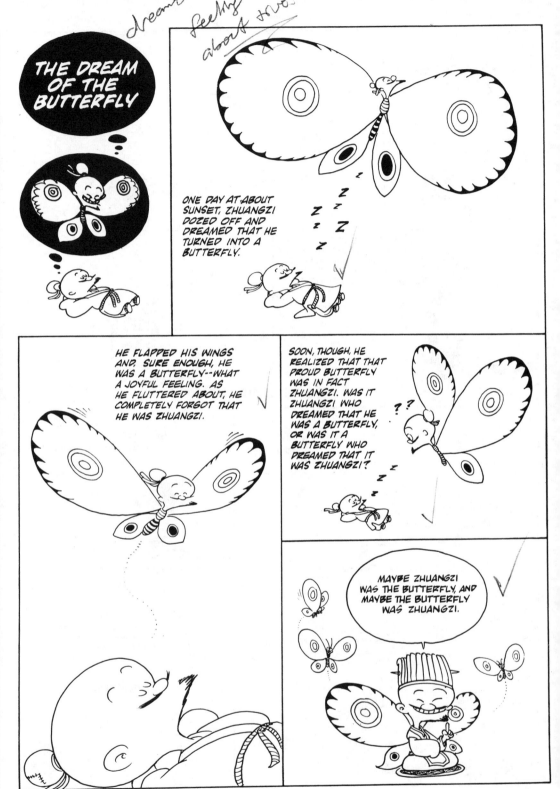

THE DREAM OF THE BUTTERFLY

ONE DAY AT ABOUT SUNSET, ZHUANGZI DOZED OFF AND DREAMED THAT HE TURNED INTO A BUTTERFLY.

HE FLAPPED HIS WINGS AND, SURE ENOUGH, HE WAS A BUTTERFLY--WHAT A JOYFUL FEELING. AS HE FLUTTERED ABOUT, HE COMPLETELY FORGOT THAT HE WAS ZHUANGZI.

SOON, THOUGH, HE REALIZED THAT THAT PROUD BUTTERFLY WAS IN FACT ZHUANGZI. WAS IT ZHUANGZI WHO DREAMED THAT HE WAS A BUTTERFLY, OR WAS IT A BUTTERFLY WHO DREAMED THAT IT WAS ZHUANGZI?

MAYBE ZHUANGZI WAS THE BUTTERFLY, AND MAYBE THE BUTTERFLY WAS ZHUANGZI.

THREE AT DAWN AND FOUR AT DUSK

Some people never get over things??

ONE MORNING, A MONKEY TRAINER BROUGHT IN A BASKET FULL OF CHESTNUTS TO FEED HIS MONKEYS.

Yes!

HE SAID TO THEM:

I'LL GIVE YOU EACH THREE IN THE MORNING AND FOUR AT NIGHT, HOW'S THAT?

RRRR!

OKAY THEN, I'LL GIVE YOU FOUR IN THE MORNING AND THREE AT NIGHT.

WHOOPIE!

YEA!

THERE'S REALLY NO DIFFERENCE BETWEEN "THREE AT DAWN AND FOUR AT DUSK" AND "FOUR AT DAWN AND THREE AT DUSK," BUT THE SIMPLE ALTERATION CONTROLLED THE MONKEYS' DELIGHT AND ANGER. DO PEOPLE EVER MAKE THE SAME MISTAKE AS THE MONKEYS? THINK ABOUT IT.

唯達者知通唯一，為是不用而寓諸庸。庸也者，用也；用也者，通也；通也者，得也；適得而幾矣。因是已。已而不知其然，謂之道。勞神明為一而不知其同也，謂之朝三。何謂朝三？

狙公賦芧，曰：「朝三而暮四，」眾狙皆怒。曰：

「然則朝四而暮三，」眾狙皆悅。名實未虧而喜怒為用，亦因是也。是以聖人和之以是非而休乎天鈞，是之謂兩行。

〔莊子⊙齊物論第二〕

27

昭文之鼓琴也，師曠之枝策也，惠子之據梧也，三子之知幾乎，皆其盛者也，故載之末年。

〔莊子◎齊物論第二〕

28

庖丁為文惠君解牛，手之所觸，肩之所倚，足之所履，膝之所踦，砉然嚮然，奏刀騞然，莫不中音。合於桑林之舞，乃中經首之會。

文惠君曰：「嘻，善哉！技蓋至此乎？」

庖丁釋刀對曰：「臣之所好者道也，進乎技矣。

始臣之解牛之時，所見无非全牛者。三年之後，未嘗見全牛也。方今之時，臣以神遇而不以目視，官知止而神欲行。依乎天理，批大卻，導大窾，因其固然。技經肯綮之未嘗，而況大軱乎！良庖歲更刀，割也；族庖月更刀，折也。今臣之刀十九年矣，所解數千牛矣，而刀刃若新發於硎。彼節者有閒，而刀刃者無厚；以無厚入有閒，恢恢乎其於遊刃必有餘地矣，是以十九年而刀刃若新發於硎。雖然，每至於族，吾見其難為，怵然為戒，視為止，行為遲。動刀甚微，謋然已解，如土委地。提刀而立，為之

四顧，為之躊躇滿志，善刀而藏之。」

文惠君曰：「善哉！吾聞庖丁之言，得養生焉。」

【莊子⊙養生主第三】

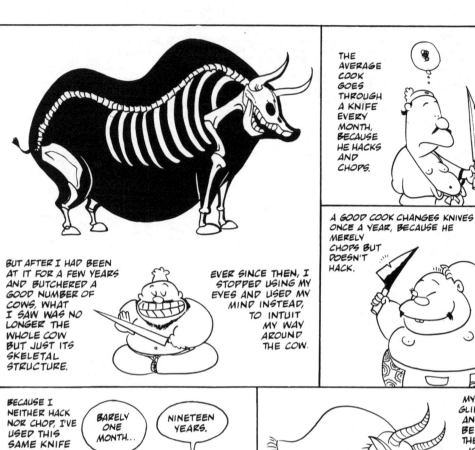

THE AVERAGE COOK GOES THROUGH A KNIFE EVERY MONTH, BECAUSE HE HACKS AND CHOPS.

A GOOD COOK CHANGES KNIVES ONCE A YEAR, BECAUSE HE MERELY CHOPS BUT DOESN'T HACK.

BUT AFTER I HAD BEEN AT IT FOR A FEW YEARS AND BUTCHERED A GOOD NUMBER OF COWS, WHAT I SAW WAS NO LONGER THE WHOLE COW BUT JUST ITS SKELETAL STRUCTURE.

EVER SINCE THEN, I STOPPED USING MY EYES AND USED MY MIND INSTEAD, TO INTUIT MY WAY AROUND THE COW.

BECAUSE I NEITHER HACK NOR CHOP, I'VE USED THIS SAME KNIFE FOR NINETEEN YEARS, AND IT'S STILL LIKE NEW.

BARELY ONE MONTH...

NINETEEN YEARS.

MY KNIFE GLIDES IN AND OUT BETWEEN THE BONE JOINTS, MOVING AS IT PLEASES; THE COW SUFFERS NO PAIN AND IN THE END DOESN'T EVEN KNOW IT'S DEAD.

FANTASTIC! WHAT YOU HAVE SAID TODAY HAS TAUGHT ME A LOT ABOUT THE "PRINCIPLE OF NURTURING LIFE."

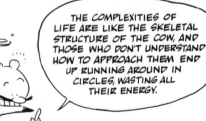

THE COMPLEXITIES OF LIFE ARE LIKE THE SKELETAL STRUCTURE OF THE COW, AND THOSE WHO DON'T UNDERSTAND HOW TO APPROACH THEM END UP RUNNING AROUND IN CIRCLES, WASTING ALL THEIR ENERGY.

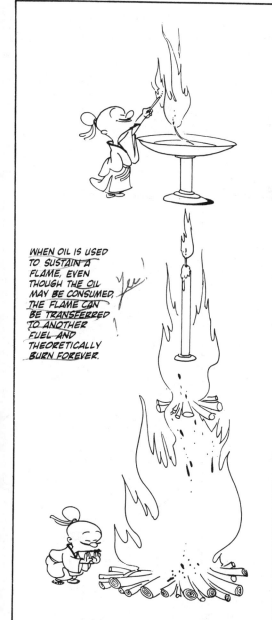

PASSING ON THE FLAME

WHEN OIL IS USED TO SUSTAIN A FLAME, EVEN THOUGH THE OIL MAY BE CONSUMED, THE FLAME CAN BE TRANSFERRED TO ANOTHER FUEL AND THEORETICALLY BURN FOREVER.

DAO!

DAO!

DAO!

DAO!

OUR BODIES WILL DIE SOMEDAY, BUT OUR SPIRIT AND THOUGHTS CAN BE PASSED ON-- FOREVER.

NURTURING LIFE DOES NOT AIM AT PRESERVING THE BODY BUT AT NOURISHING THE SPIRIT, ALLOWING IT TO LIVE FOREVER.

指窮於為薪，火傳也，不知其盡也。

【莊子◉養生主第三】

31

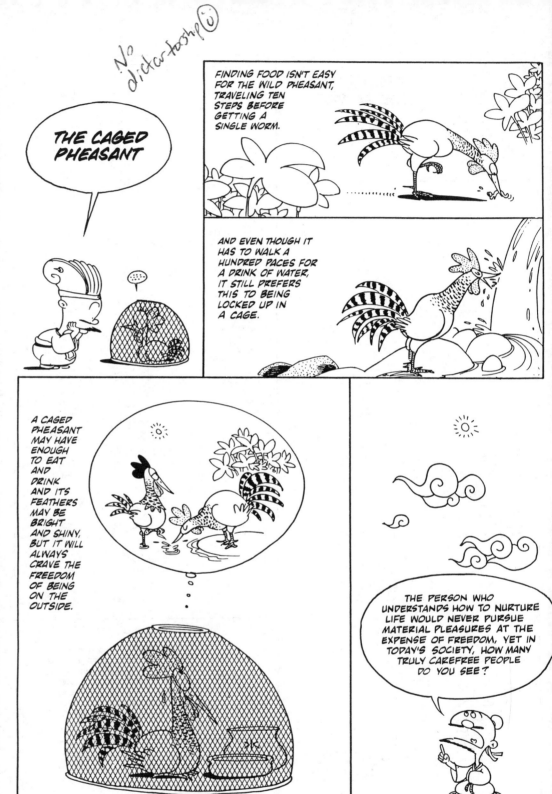

No dictatorship

THE CAGED PHEASANT

FINDING FOOD ISN'T EASY FOR THE WILD PHEASANT, TRAVELING TEN STEPS BEFORE GETTING A SINGLE WORM.

AND EVEN THOUGH IT HAS TO WALK A HUNDRED PACES FOR A DRINK OF WATER, IT STILL PREFERS THIS TO BEING LOCKED UP IN A CAGE.

A CAGED PHEASANT MAY HAVE ENOUGH TO EAT AND DRINK AND ITS FEATHERS MAY BE BRIGHT AND SHINY, BUT IT WILL ALWAYS CRAVE THE FREEDOM OF BEING ON THE OUTSIDE.

THE PERSON WHO UNDERSTANDS HOW TO NURTURE LIFE WOULD NEVER PURSUE MATERIAL PLEASURES AT THE EXPENSE OF FREEDOM, YET IN TODAY'S SOCIETY, HOW MANY TRULY CAREFREE PEOPLE DO YOU SEE?

LIKE A MANTIS STOPPING A CART

THERE WAS A MAN NAMED YAN HE, WHO WAS ABOUT TO GO ON A MISSION TO PERSUADE THE EVIL PRINCE FU TO CHANGE HIS WAYS. BEFORE LEAVING, HE WENT TO QU BOYU FOR ADVICE.

THERE IS A PERSON WHO IS A KILLER BY NATURE. IF LEFT TO HIS OWN DEVICES, HE WILL BRING HARM UPON THE NATION.

why?

AND IF ONE ATTEMPTS TO PERSUADE HIM OTHERWISE, HE WILL BRING HARM UPON THE PERSUADER.

dirty to chope him

THIS PERSON SEES ONLY THE FAULTS OF OTHERS AND IS BLIND TO HIS OWN SHORTCOMINGS. WHAT CAN BE DONE?

IN DEALING WITH THIS TYPE OF PERSON, YOU MUST FIRST BE FLEXIBLE AND CONFORM TO HIS BEHAVIOR. DON'T ANGER HIM.

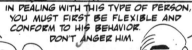

IF HE ACTS LIKE A CHILD, YOU ACT LIKE A CHILD.

IF HE ACTS LIKE A LUNATIC, YOU ACT LIKE A LUNATIC.

HA HA HA!

HA HA HA!

顏闔將傅衛靈公大子，而問於蘧伯玉曰：「有人於此，其德天殺。與之為無方，則危吾國；與之為有方，則危吾身。其知適足以知人之過，而不知其所以過。若然者，吾奈之何？」

蘧伯玉曰：「善哉問乎！戒之，慎之，正女身也哉！形莫若就，心莫若和。雖然，之二者有患。就不欲入，和不欲出。形就而入，且為顛為滅，為崩為蹶。心和而出，且為聲為名，為妖為孽。彼且為嬰兒，亦與之為嬰兒；彼且為無町畦，亦與之為無町畦；彼且為無崖，亦與之為無崖。達之，入於無

33

疵。汝不知夫螳螂乎？怒其臂以當車轍，不知其不勝任也，是其才之美者也。戒之，慎之，積伐而美者以犯之，幾矣。」

匠石之齊，至於曲轅，見櫟社樹。其大蔽數千牛，絜之百圍，其高臨山十仞而後有枝，其可以為舟者旁十數。觀者如市，匠伯不顧，遂行不輟。弟子厭觀之，走及匠石，曰：「自吾執斧斤以隨夫子，未嘗見材如此其美也。先生不肯視，行不輟，何邪？」

曰：「已矣，勿言之矣！散木也，以為舟則沈，以為棺槨則速腐，以為器則速毀，以為門戶則液樠，以為柱則蠹。是不材之木也，無所可用，故能若是之壽。」

THE EARTH SPIRIT'S TREE

A MASTER CARPENTER WAS TAKING HIS STUDENTS TO THE STATE OF QI TO BUILD A HOUSE.

ON THE WAY, THEY PASSED A TREE STANDING BESIDE A TEMPLE TO THE EARTH SPIRIT. THE TREE WAS GIGANTIC BEYOND COMPARE. ITS TRUNK WAS HUGE, AND IT WAS SO TALL THAT IT ALMOST TOUCHED THE CLOUDS.

HMPH!

?

MASTER!

HEY, THAT'S THE BIGGEST TREE WE'VE EVER SEEN. HOW COME YOU DIDN'T EVEN STOP AND TAKE A LOOK?

HMPH!

FORGET IT. THAT THING IS COMPLETELY USELESS.

HMPH!

匠石歸，櫟社見夢曰：「女將惡乎比予哉？若將比予於文木邪？夫柤梨橘柚，果蓏之屬，實熟則剝，剝則辱；大枝折，小枝泄。此以其能苦其生者也，故不終其天年而中道夭，自掊擊於世俗者也。物莫不若是。且予求无所可用久矣，幾死，乃今得之，為予大用。使予也而有用，且得有此大也邪？且也若與予也皆物也，奈何哉其相物也？而幾死之散人，又惡知散木！」

【莊子●人間世第四】

宋有荊氏者，宜楸柏桑。其拱把而上者，求狙猴
之杙者斬之；三圍四圍，求高名之麗者斬之；七圍
八圍，貴人富商之家求樿傍者斬之。故未終其天年，
而中道之夭於斧斤，此材之患也。故解之牛之白顙
者與豚之亢鼻者，與人有痔病者不可以適河。此皆
巫祝以知之矣，所以為不祥也。此乃神人之所以為
大祥也。

【莊子◉人間世第四】

A TREE'S NATURAL LIFE SPAN

IN SONG, THERE WAS A PLACE THAT WAS WELL SUITED FOR GROWING JAPONICA, CYPRESS, AND MULBERRY TREES. WHEN THESE TREES GREW TO A CERTAIN WIDTH, THEY WERE CUT DOWN AND USED TO BUILD MONKEY CAGES.

THE THICKER ONES WERE USED TO BUILD TALL HOUSES.

福

IF EVEN THICKER, THEY WERE CUT DOWN AND USED TO MAKE COFFINS FOR THE RICH.

NONE OF THESE TREES EVER LIVED TO ENJOY A FULL NATURAL LIFE SPAN, AND INSTEAD WERE CUT DOWN IN THE PRIME OF LIFE.

THOSE POOR USEFUL TREES...

IN ANCIENT TIMES, DURING THE SACRIFICE TO THE RIVER GOD, THE SHAMAN WOULD NEVER CHOOSE A COW WITH A WHITE FOREHEAD, A PIG WITH A LONG SNOUT, OR A PERSON WITH HEMORRHOIDS TO THROW INTO THE RIVER AS A SACRIFICE. THEY WERE CONSIDERED TO BE "INAUSPICIOUS."

I HAVE HEMORRHOIDS.

I HAVE A LONG SNOUT.

INAUSPICIOUS CREATURES...

I HAVE A WHITE FOREHEAD.

THE INTELLIGENT AND VERSATILE PERSON WOULD PRETEND TO BE UNFIT, OR INAUSPICIOUS, IN ORDER TO AVOID THIS SPIRITUAL DISASTER.

INAUSPICIOUS

INAUSPICIOUS

INAUSPICIOUS

BEAUTIFUL AND UGLY EACH HAVE THEIR OWN SPECIAL CHARACTERISTICS. IT'S NOT NECESSARY TO DISTINGUISH BETWEEN "GOOD" AND "BAD" AND "AUSPICIOUS" AND "INAUSPICIOUS."

IF A WOMAN IS CHOSEN TO BE SACRIFICED TO THE RIVER GOD BECAUSE OF HER BEAUTY, THEN IS BEAUTY AUSPICIOUS OR INAUSPICIOUS?

AUSPICIOUS?

INAUSPICIOUS?

宋有荊氏者，宜楸柏桑。其拱把而上者，求狙猴之杙者斬之；三圍四圍，求高名之麗者斬之；七圍八圍，貴人富商之家求樿傍者斬之。故未終其天年，而中道之夭於斧斤，此材之患也。故解之牛之白顙者與豚之亢鼻者，與人有痔病者不可以適河。此皆巫祝以知之矣，所以為不祥也。此乃神人之所以為大祥也。

【莊子●人間世第四】

39

支離疏者，頤隱於臍，肩高於頂，會撮指天，五管在上，兩髀為脅，挫鍼治繲，足以餬口；鼓筴播精，足以食十人。上徵武士，則支離攘臂而遊於其間；上有大役，則支離以有常疾不受功；上與病者粟，則受三鍾與十束薪。夫支離其形者，猶足以養其身，終其天年，又況支離其德者乎！

【莊子◉人間世第四】

THE FREAK

THERE WAS ONCE A VERY PECULIAR MAN NAMED ZHI LISHU WHOSE BODY WAS TERRIBLY DEFORMED. HIS HEAD WAS BENT DOWN BELOW HIS NAVEL, HIS SHOULDERS REACHED UP ABOVE THE TOP OF HIS HEAD, HIS HAIR STUCK OUT IN ALL DIRECTIONS, HIS VITAL ORGANS WERE ALL OUT OF PLACE, AND HIS STOMACH HUNG DOWN BETWEEN HIS THIGHS.

BY HELPING PEOPLE WITH THEIR LAUNDRY, ZHI LISHU COULD MAKE ENOUGH MONEY TO GET BY.

VERY LUCKY, VERY LUCKY.

AND BY TELLING FORTUNES, HE COULD SUPPORT A DOZEN PEOPLE.

DURING TIMES OF WAR WHEN PEOPLE WERE CONSCRIPTED BY FORCE, ZHI LISHU SAUNTERED DOWN THE STREET KNOWING THAT NOBODY WOULD WANT HIM.

HUMBY DEE DUM DUM.

DURING TIMES OF FAMINE WHEN THE GOVERNMENT GAVE OUT FREE GRAIN, ZHI LISHU WOULD BE FIRST IN LINE DUE TO HIS DISABILITY.

THE WISE PERSON DOESN'T CARE ABOUT UNAPPEALING ASPECTS OR DISABILITIES. THESE ATTRIBUTES CAN ALSO SAVE ONE FROM MUCH GRIEF AND HARDSHIP.

RIGHT!

positive in everything

41

〔莊子⊙人間世第四〕

汝不知夫養虎者乎？不敢以生物與之，為其殺之之怒也；不敢以全物與之，為其決之之怒也；時其飢飽，達其怒心。虎之與人異類而媚養己者，順也；故其殺者，逆也。

Think on the
bright side/things in yourself!

TOELESS SHU

THERE WAS ONCE A MAN IN LU BY THE NAME OF TOELESS SHU SHAN. TOELESS SHU HAD HAD HIS TOES CHOPPED OFF FOR COMMITTING A CRIME.

ONE DAY, HE WALKED ON HIS STUMPS TO GO SEE CONFUCIUS.

IT'S BECAUSE YOU DIDN'T CARE ABOUT YOUR OWN WELL-BEING THAT YOU HAD YOUR TOES CUT OFF. IT'S TOO LATE TO CHANGE THAT NOW.

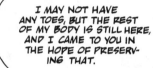

I MAY NOT HAVE ANY TOES, BUT THE REST OF MY BODY IS STILL HERE, AND I CAME TO YOU IN THE HOPE OF PRESERVING THAT.

HMPH!

I APOLOGIZE.

YOU ARE A WISE MAN. PLEASE COME IN AND TEACH MY DISCIPLES.

TOELESS SHU SHAN WAS A MAN OF HIGH VIRTUE, AND THAT IS WHY CONFUCIUS CHANGED HIS ATTITUDE TOWARD HIM. A SIMPLE DISABILITY DOES NOT MAKE ONE A CRIPPLE.

BUT TOELESS SHU HAD ALREADY STARTED ON HIS WAY.

魯有兀者叔山无趾，踵見仲尼。仲尼曰：「子不謹，前既犯患若是矣。雖今來，何及矣！」

无趾曰：「吾唯不知務而輕用吾身，吾是以亡足。今吾來也，猶有尊足者存，吾是以務全之也。夫天無不覆，地無不載，吾以夫子為天地，安知夫子之猶若是也！」

孔子曰：「丘則陋矣。夫子胡不入乎，請講以所聞！」

无趾出。孔子曰：「弟子勉之！夫无趾，兀者也，猶務學以復補前行之惡，而況全德之人乎！」

【莊子⊙德充符第五】

43

泉涸，魚相與處於陸，相呴以濕，相濡以沫，不如相忘於江湖。與其譽堯而非桀也，不如兩忘而化其道。夫大塊載我以形，勞我以生，佚我以老，息我以死。故善吾生者，乃所以善吾死也。

【莊子◎大宗師第六】

NATURE THE SUPERHERO

NATURE IS LIKE A SUPERHERO, ITS LIMITLESS STRENGTH CONTINUALLY PULSING.

NATURE GAVE ME MY BODY,

GAVE ME VITALITY SO THAT I CAN WORK HARD,

GAVE ME AGE SO THAT I CAN GROW OLD IN EASE AND COMFORT,

AND GAVE ME DEATH SO THAT I CAN HAVE EVERLASTING PEACE.

NATURE IS CONSTANTLY CHANGING, AND PEOPLE HAVE TO ACKNOWLEDGE AND ADAPT TO THESE CHANGES. THIS WAY, REACTIONS OF DELIGHT AND FEAR WILL DISSIPATE, AND THE DISTINCTION BETWEEN LIFE AND DEATH WILL LOSE ITS SIGNIFICANCE.

ZI SANG QUESTIONS HIS FATE

子輿與子桑友，而霖雨十日。子輿曰：「子桑殆病矣！」裹飯而往食之。至子桑之門，則若歌若哭，鼓琴曰：「父邪！母邪！天乎！人乎！」有不任其聲而趨舉其詩焉。子輿入，曰：「子之歌詩，何故若是？」

曰：「吾思夫使我至此極者而弗得也。父母豈欲吾貧哉？天無私覆，地無私載，天地豈私貧我哉？求其為之者而不得也。然而至此極者，命也夫！」

【莊子⊙大宗師第六】

駢於辯者，累瓦結繩竄句，遊心於堅白同異之間……

而敝跬譽無用之言非乎？而楊墨是已。故此皆多

駢旁枝之道，非天下之至正也。

彼正正者，不失其性命之情。故合者不為駢，而

枝者不為跂；長者不為有餘，短者不為不足。是故

鳧脛雖短，續之則憂；鶴脛雖長，斷之則悲。故性

長非所斷，性短非所續，無所去憂也。意仁義其非

人情乎！彼仁人何其多憂也？

【莊子⊙駢拇第八】

ARE A DUCK'S LEGS TOO SHORT?

NATURALLY LONG COULDN'T BE TOO LONG, AND SHORT COULDN'T BE TOO SHORT.

ALTHOUGH A DUCK'S LEGS ARE VERY SHORT, IT CERTAINLY WOULDN'T WANT THEM LENGTHENED.

!

AND ALTHOUGH A CRANE'S LEGS ARE VERY LONG, IT WOULD BE OUTRAGED IF THEY WERE SHORTENED.

!

A DUCK'S LEGS ARE SHORT, BUT ITS NECK IS LONG.

ISN'T THIS CONVENIENT?

AND A CRANE'S LEGS ARE LONG, WHILE ITS NECK IS SHORT. SO IN THE END, EVERYTHING IS AS IT SHOULD BE.

TRY NOT TO DISTINGUISH LONG AND SHORT ACCORDING TO HUMAN STANDARDS. INSTEAD, OBSERVE THEIR FUNCTIONS IN NATURE, AND YOU'LL SEE THAT LONG IS NO LONGER LONG AND SHORT IS NO LONGER SHORT.

故跖之徒問於跖曰：「盜亦有道乎？」跖曰：「何適而無有道邪！」夫妄意室中之藏，聖也；入先，勇也；出後，義也；知可否，知也；分均，仁也。五者不備而能成大盜者，天下未之有也。由是觀之，善人不得聖人之道不立，跖不得聖人之道不行

：天下之善人少而不善人多，則聖人之利天下也少而害天下也多。

【莊子○胠篋第十】

故曰，脣竭則齒寒，魯酒薄而邯鄲圍，聖人生而大盜起。掊擊聖人，縱舍盜賊，而天下始治矣。夫川竭而谷虛，丘夷而淵實。聖人已死，則大盜不起，天下平而無故矣。

許慎注淮南云：楚會諸侯，魯趙俱獻酒於楚王。楚之主酒過求酒於趙，趙不與。更怒，乃以趙厚酒易魯薄酒，奏之。楚王以趙酒薄，故圍邯鄲也。

【莊子◎胠篋第十】

52

Theres
an inbetween
of good & bad

THE YELLOW EMPEROR QUESTIONS GUANGCHENG

WHEN THE YELLOW EMPEROR HAD BEEN REIGNING FOR NINETEEN YEARS AND HAD BROUGHT CIVILIZATION TO THE LAND, HE HEARD ABOUT AN ENLIGHT-ENED MASTER NAMED GUANGCHENGZI. OUT OF CURIOSITY, THE EMPEROR WENT TO SEE HIM.

??

I WANT TO USE THE VITALITY OF NATURE TO HARMONIZE THE YIN AND THE YANG; THIS WILL BRING UNPRECEDENTED HARVESTS. I WANT TO HELP MY PEOPLE CULTIVATE THEIR ORIGINAL NATURE...

YOU SAY YOU WANT TO USE THE VITALITY OF THE DAO TO ENHANCE THE NAT-URAL PROCESSES? THIS WILL ONLY DE-STROY THEM. DON'T YOU UNDERSTAND THAT TO USE OUR INTELLECT TO CHANGE THINGS ONLY MAKES MATTERS WORSE?

UPON HEARING THIS, THE KING'S PASSION TURNED TO DUST AND HE IMMEDIATELY ABDICATED. HE LEFT THE WORLD BEHIND AND WENT TO LIVE BY HIMSELF IN A GRASS HUT. HE STAYED THERE IN PEACE AND SOLITUDE FOR THREE MONTHS.

HOW SHOULD I GOVERN MY BODY THAT I MAY LIVE A LONG LIFE?

medium?

THE DAO IS CHAOTIC, NEITHER BRIGHT NOR DARK.

DON'T SEE WITH YOUR EYES, DON'T HEAR WITH YOUR EARS, DON'T THINK WITH YOUR MIND, EMBRACE THE PRIMAL ONE, NO KNOWLEDGE, NO SELF, GO WITH NATURE, PARTICIPATE IN NATURE, BE ONE WITH NATURE, AND A LONG LIFE WILL COME NATURALLY.

（上略）

黃帝退，捐天下，築特室，席白茅，閒居三月，復往邀之。

廣成子南首而臥，黃帝順下風膝行而進，再拜稽首而問曰：「聞君子達於至道，敢問，治身奈何而可以長久？」廣成子蹶然而起，曰：「善哉問乎！來！吾語女至道。至道之精，窈窈冥冥；至道之極，昏昏默默。無視無聽，抱神以靜，形將自正。必靜必清，无勞女形，无搖女精，乃可以長生。」

【莊子⊙在宥第十一】

夫有土者，有大物也。有大物者，不可以物；物而不物，故能物物。明乎物物者之非物也，豈獨治天下百姓而已哉！出入六合，遊乎九州，獨往獨來，是謂獨有。獨有之人，是謂至貴。

大人之教，若形之於影，聲之於響。有問而應之，盡其所懷，為天下配。處乎无響，行乎无方。挈汝適復之撓撓，以遊无端；出入无旁，與日无始；頌論形軀，合乎大同，大同而无己。无己，惡乎得有有！覩有者，昔之君子；覩无者，天地之友。

【莊子◉在宥第十一】

桓公讀書於堂上。輪扁斲輪於堂下，釋椎鑿而上問桓公曰：「敢問，公之所讀者何言邪？」

公曰：「聖人之言也。」

曰：「聖人在乎？」

公曰：「已死矣。」

曰：「然則君子所讀者，古人之糟魄已夫！」

桓公曰：「寡人讀書，輪人安得議乎！有說則可，无說則死。」

輪扁曰：「臣也以臣之事觀之。斲輪，徐則甘而不固，疾則苦而不入。不徐不疾，得之於手而應於

THE SECRET TO WHEEL MAKING IS A CHISEL THAT IS NEITHER SLOW NOR FAST, BUT ONE THAT MOVES EXACTLY AS YOU WISH IT.

I CAN EXPLAIN THIS TO MY SON, BUT I CAN'T PASS ON THE SKILL TO HIM, AND THAT IS WHY AT SEVENTY YEARS OLD, I AM STILL MAKING WHEELS.

SO YOU SEE, THE WISDOM OF ANCIENT SAGES CAN'T BE PASSED DOWN, AND THAT'S WHY I SAY THE BOOK YOU'RE READING IS MERELY THE DREGS OF A DEAD MAN.

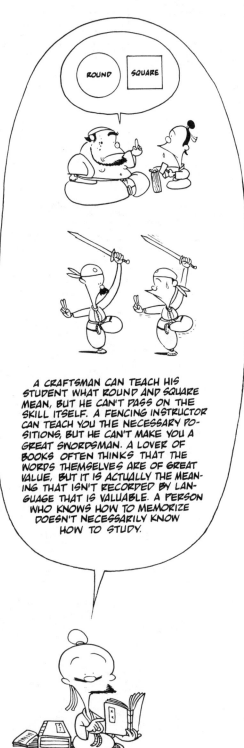

ROUND SQUARE

A CRAFTSMAN CAN TEACH HIS STUDENT WHAT ROUND AND SQUARE MEAN, BUT HE CAN'T PASS ON THE SKILL ITSELF. A FENCING INSTRUCTOR CAN TEACH YOU THE NECESSARY POSITIONS, BUT HE CAN'T MAKE YOU A GREAT SWORDSMAN. A LOVER OF BOOKS OFTEN THINKS THAT THE WORDS THEMSELVES ARE OF GREAT VALUE, BUT IT IS ACTUALLY THE MEANING THAT ISN'T RECORDED BY LANGUAGE THAT IS VALUABLE. A PERSON WHO KNOWS HOW TO MEMORIZE DOESN'T NECESSARILY KNOW HOW TO STUDY.

THE EARTH AND THE SKY

天其運乎？地其處乎？日月其爭於所乎？孰主張是？孰維綱是？孰居无事推而行事？意者其有機緘而不得已邪？意者其運轉而不能自止邪？雲者為雨乎？雨者為雲乎？孰隆施是？孰居无事淫樂而勸是？風起北方，一西一東，有上彷徨，孰噓吸是？孰居无事而披拂是？敢問何故？

【莊子◉天運第十四】

孔子見老聃而語仁義。老聃曰：「夫播穅眯目，則天地四方易位矣；蚊蝱噆膚，則通昔不寐矣。夫仁義憯然乃憤吾心，亂莫大焉。吾子使天下无失其朴，吾子亦放風而動，總德而立矣。又奚傑然若負建鼓而求亡子者邪？夫鵠不日浴而白，烏不日黔而黑。黑白之朴，不足以為辯；名譽之觀，不足以為廣。」

CONFUCIUS SEES A DRAGON

AFTER HIS MEETING WITH LAOZI, CONFUCIUS RETURNED HOME AND DIDN'T SPEAK FOR THREE DAYS.

MASTER, WHEN YOU WENT TO SEE LAOZI WHAT DID YOU TEACH HIM?

UM, UM, UM...

I SAW A DRAGON, FLOWING WITH THE YIN AND YANG, CEASELESSLY CHANGING. I OPENED MY MOUTH, BUT NO SOUND CAME OUT. WHAT COULD I POSSIBLY TEACH HIM?

CONFUCIUS KNEW THAT LAOZI UNDERSTOOD THE WAY OF NATURE--CEASELESS TRANSFORMATION. WHEN FACING A PERSON WHO UNDERSTANDS THE DAO, WORDS ARE USELESS AND UNNECESSARY.

孔子見老耼歸，三日不談。弟子問曰：「夫子見老耼，亦將何規哉？」
孔子曰：「吾乃今於是乎見龍！龍，合而成體，散而成章，乘雲氣而養乎陰陽予口張而不能嗋，予又何規老耼哉！」

【莊子◉天運第十四】

59

河伯曰：「何謂天？何謂人？」

北海若曰：「牛馬四足，是謂天；落馬首，穿牛鼻，是謂人。

故曰，无以人滅天；无以故滅命，无以得殉名。

謹守而勿失，是謂反其真。」

【莊子⊙秋水第十七】

DON'T RING THE BULL'S NOSE

ONE DAY, THE LORD OF THE YELLOW RIVER ASKED THE SEA SPIRIT:

WHAT IS NATURAL AND WHAT IS MAN-MADE?

FOUR LEGS ON HORSES AND COWS IS NATURAL.

A HORSE'S HARNESS...

...AND A BULL'S NOSE RING ARE MAN-MADE.

MAN-MADE KNOWLEDGE, MORALITY, AND LAWS ALL WORK AGAINST NATURE, JUST LIKE A HORSE'S HARNESS AND A BULL'S NOSE-RING.

everybody has there own use and own purpose for living so don't judge

蓬蓬然起於北海，蓬蓬然入於南海，而似无有，何也？」

風曰：「然。予蓬蓬然起於北海而入於南海也，然而指我則勝我，鰌我亦勝我。雖然，夫折大木，蜚大屋者，唯我能也，故以眾小不勝為大勝也。為大勝者，唯聖人能之。」

COURAGE OF THE SAGE

ONE DAY WHEN CONFUCIUS WAS ON *A JOURNEY WITH* HIS DISCIPLES IN ZHOU, HE WAS SURROUNDED BY A POSSE WHO MISTOOK HIM FOR THE REBEL YANG HU.

DON'T PANIC, JUST SIT STILL AND CONTINUE LISTENING TO ME TEACH.

BUT AREN'T YOU AFRAID, MASTER?

OF COURSE I AM, ZHONG YOU, BUT LISTEN...

NOT TO FEAR WATER DRAGONS IS THE COURAGE OF THE FISHERMAN.

孔子遊於匡，宋人圍之數帀，而絃歌不惙。子路入見，曰：「何夫子之娛也？」孔子曰：「來！吾語女。我諱窮久矣，而不免，命也；求通久矣，而不得，時也。當堯舜而天下無窮人，非知得也；當桀紂而天下無通人，非知失也；時勢適然。夫水行不避蛟龍者，漁父之勇也；陸行不避兕虎者，獵夫之勇也；白刃交於前，視死若生者，烈士之勇也；知窮之有命，知通之有時，臨大難而不懼者，聖人之勇也。由處矣，吾命有所制矣。」无幾何，將甲者進，辭曰：「以為陽虎也，窮人，非知窮也；

63

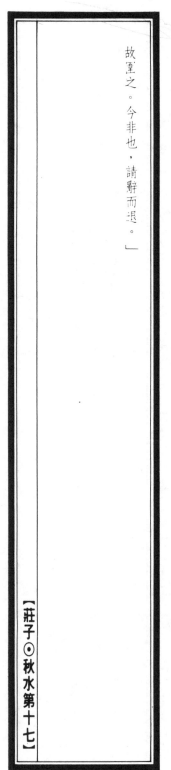

公孫龍問於魏牟曰：「龍少學先生之道，長而明
仁義之行；合同異，離堅白；然不然，可不可；困
百家之知，窮眾口之辯；吾自以為至達已。今吾聞
莊子之言，汒焉異之。不知論之不及與，知之弗若
與？今吾无所開吾喙，敢問其方。」

公子牟隱樣大息，仰天而笑曰：「
子獨不聞夫坎井之鼃乎？謂東海之鱉曰：『吾樂
與！出跳梁乎井幹之上，入休乎缺甃之崖；赴水則
接腋持頤，蹶泥則沒足滅跗；還虷蟹與科斗，莫吾
能若也。且夫擅一壑之水，而跨跱坎井選樂，此亦

至矣，夫子奚不時來入觀乎！」東海之鱉左足未入，而右膝已縶矣。於是逡巡而卻，告之海曰：『夫千里之遠，不足以舉其大；千仞之高，不足以極其深。禹之時十年九潦，而水弗為加益；湯之時八年七旱，而崖不為加損。夫不為頃久推移，不以多少

進退者，此亦東海之大樂也。」於是埳井之䵷聞之，適適然驚，規規然自失也。

且夫知不知是非之竟，而猶欲觀於莊子之言，是猶使蚊負山，商蚷馳河也，必不勝任矣。且夫知不知論極妙之言而自適一時之利者，是非埳井之龜與

且彼方跐黄泉而登大皇，无南无北，奭然四解，淪於不測；无東无西，始於玄冥，反於大通。子乃規規然而求之以察，索之以辯，是直用管闚天，用錐指地也，不亦小乎！子往矣！且子獨不聞夫壽陵餘子之學行於邯鄲與？未得國能，又失其故行矣，直匍匐而歸耳。今子不去，將忘子之故，失子之業餘子之？」

【莊子◉秋水第十七】

且子獨不聞夫壽陵餘子之學行於邯鄲與？未得國

能，又失其故行矣，直匍匐而歸耳。

【莊子⊙秋水第十七】

LEARNING
HOW
TO
WALK
IN
HANDAN

THERE WAS ONCE A LITTLE BOY FROM YAN WHO WENT TO THE CITY OF HANDAN TO LEARN HOW TO WALK LIKE THE PEOPLE THERE.

BUT NOT ONLY DID HE NOT LEARN HOW TO WALK THERE, HE FORGOT HOW TO WALK ALTOGETHER!

AH! I CAN'T WALK!

SO HE HAD TO CRAWL HOME.

AT THE OUTSET, PEOPLE WHO STUDY ARE IN SEARCH OF THE ESSENCE OF NATURE, BUT AFTER A WHILE THEY GET LOST IN THE FOREST OF BOOKS AND CAN'T GET OUT.

惠子相梁，莊子往見之。或謂惠子曰：「莊子來，欲代子相。」於是惠子恐，搜於國中三日三夜。

莊子往見之，曰：「南方有鳥，其名為鵷鶵，子知之乎？夫鵷鶵，發於南海而飛於北海，非梧桐不止，非練實不食，非醴泉不飲。於是鴟得腐鼠，鵷

鶵過之，仰而視之曰：『嚇！』今子欲以子之梁國

而嚇我邪？」

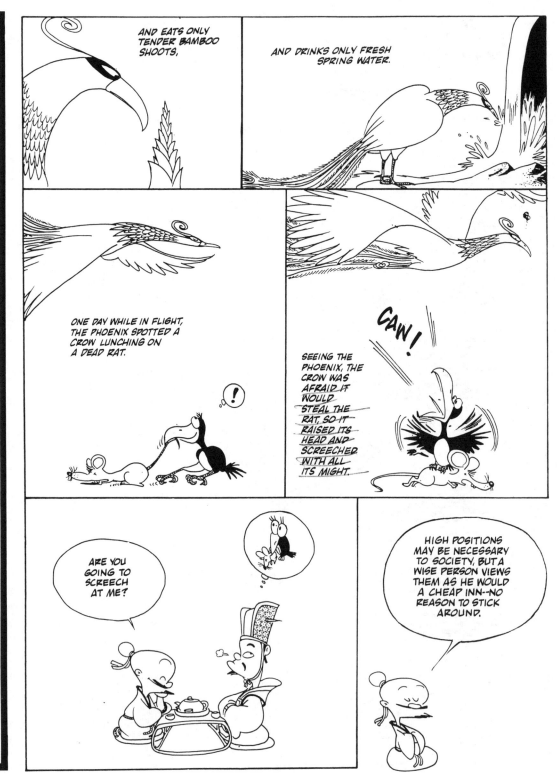

莊子之楚，見空髑髏，髐然有形，撽以馬捶，因而問之，曰：「夫子貪生失理，而為此乎？將子有亡國之事，斧鉞之誅，而為此乎？將子有不善之行，愧遺父母妻子之醜，而為此乎？將子有凍餒之患，而為此乎？將子之春秋故及此乎？」

於是語卒，援髑髏，枕而臥。夜半，髑髏見夢曰：「子之談者似辯士。視子所言，皆生人之累也，死則无此矣。子欲聞死之說乎？」

莊子曰：「然。」

髑髏曰：「死，无君於上，无臣於下；亦无四時

【莊子◎秋水第十七】

昔者海鳥止於魯郊，魯侯御而觴之于廟，奏九韶以為樂，具太牢以為膳。鳥乃眩視憂悲，不敢食一臠，不敢飲一杯，三日而死。此以己養養鳥也，非以鳥養養鳥也。夫以鳥養養鳥者，宜栖之深林，遊之壇陸，浮之江湖，食之鰌鰍，隨行列而止，委虵而處。彼唯人言之惡聞，奚以夫譊譊為乎！咸池九韶之樂，張之洞庭之野，鳥聞之而飛，獸聞之而走，魚聞之而下入，人卒聞之，相與還而觀之。魚處水而生，人處水而死，彼必相與異，其好惡故異也。故先聖不一其能，不同其事。名止於實，義設於適

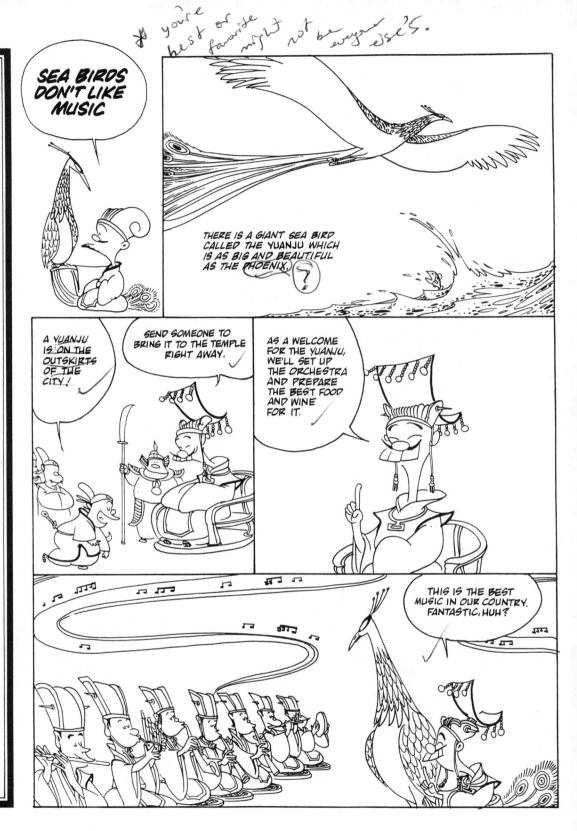

是之謂條達而福持。

【莊子◉至樂第十八】

莊子行於山中，見大木，枝葉盛茂，伐木者止其旁而不取也。問其故，曰：「无所可用。」莊子曰：「此木以不材得終其天年。」

夫子出於山，舍於故人之家。故人喜，命豎子殺雁而烹之。豎子請曰：「其一能鳴，其一不能鳴，請奚殺？」主人曰：「殺不能鳴者。」

明日，弟子問於莊子曰：「昨日山中之木，以不材得終其天年；今主人之雁，以不材死；先生將何處？」

莊子笑曰：「周將處乎材與不材之間。材與不材

77

之間，似之而非也，故未免乎累。若夫乘道德而浮
遊則不然。无譽无訾，一龍一蛇，與時俱化，而无
肯專為；一上一下，以和為量，浮遊乎萬物之祖；
物物而不物於物，則故可得而累邪！此神農黃帝之
法則也。若夫萬物之情，人倫之傳，則不然。合則

離，成則毀；廉則挫，尊則議，有為則虧，賢則謀，
不肖則欺，故可得而必乎哉！悲夫！弟子志之，其
唯道德之鄉乎！」

【莊子⊙山木第二十】

孔子圍於陳蔡之間，七日不火食。大公任往弔之曰：「子幾死乎？」曰：「然。」「子惡死乎？」曰：「然。」任曰：「予嘗言不死之道。東海有鳥焉，其名曰意怠。其為鳥也，翂翂翐翐，而似无能；引援而飛，迫脅而棲；進不敢為前，退不敢後；食不敢先嘗，必取其緒。是故其行列不斥，而外人卒不得害，是以免於患。直木先伐，甘井先竭。子其意者飾知以驚愚，脩身以明汙，昭昭乎如揭日月而行，故不免也。昔吾聞之大成之人曰：『自伐者无功，功

【莊子◎山木第二十】

成者墮，名成者虧。」孰能去功與名而還與眾人！

道流而不明，居得而不名處；純純常常，乃比於狂

；削跡捐勢，不為功名，是故无責於人，人亦无責

焉。至人不聞，子何喜哉？」

孔子曰：「善哉！」辭其交遊，去其弟子，逃於

大澤：衣裘褐，食杼栗，入獸不亂群，入鳥不亂行

。鳥獸不惡，而況人乎！

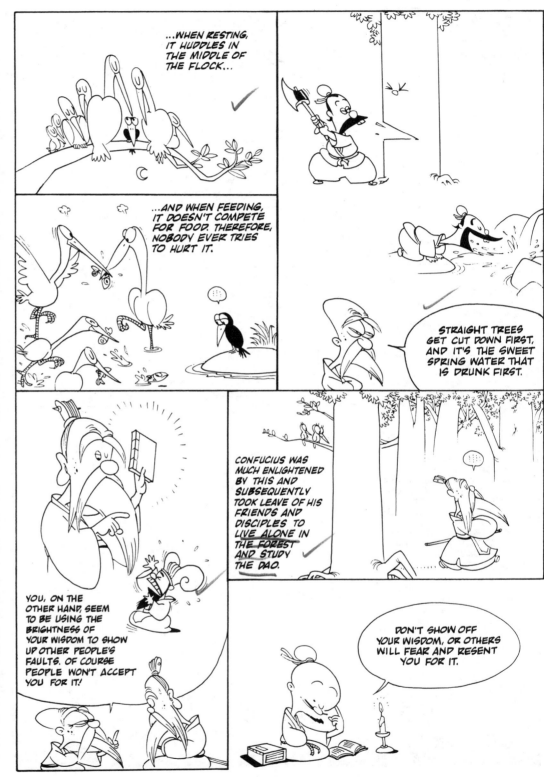

LIN HUI FORSAKES A FORTUNE

WHEN THE STATE OF JIA WAS BEING CONQUERED...

OUR NATION'S BEEN OVERRUN! WE MUST ESCAPE!

!

FORGET IT! LET'S GO!

LIN HUI GRABBED HIS CHILDREN AND RAN, LEAVING BEHIND THE FAMILY FORTUNE.

WHAT IS GAINED BY ASSESSING COST AND BENEFIT IS LOST IN THE SAME WAY. IN A WAR-TORN WORLD, PRECIOUS OBJECTS INVITE DANGER, AND AVOIDING DANGER IS A PARENT'S HIGHEST PRIORITY.

子獨不聞假人之亡與？林回棄千金之璧，負赤子而趨。或曰：『為其布與？赤子之布寡矣；為其累與？赤子之累多矣；棄千金之璧，負赤子而趨，何也？』林回曰：『彼以利合，此以天屬也。』夫以利合者，迫窮禍患害相棄也；以天屬者，迫窮禍患害相收也。夫相收之與相棄亦遠矣。

【莊子◉山木第二十】

81

【莊子◎山木第二十】

其畏人也，而襲諸人間，社稷存焉爾。

「何謂无受人益難？」

仲尼曰：「始用四達，爵祿並至而不窮，物之所利，乃非己也，吾命其在外者也。君子不為盜，賢人不為竊。吾若取之，何哉！故曰，鳥莫知於鷾鴯，目之所不宜處，不給視，雖落其實，棄之而走。

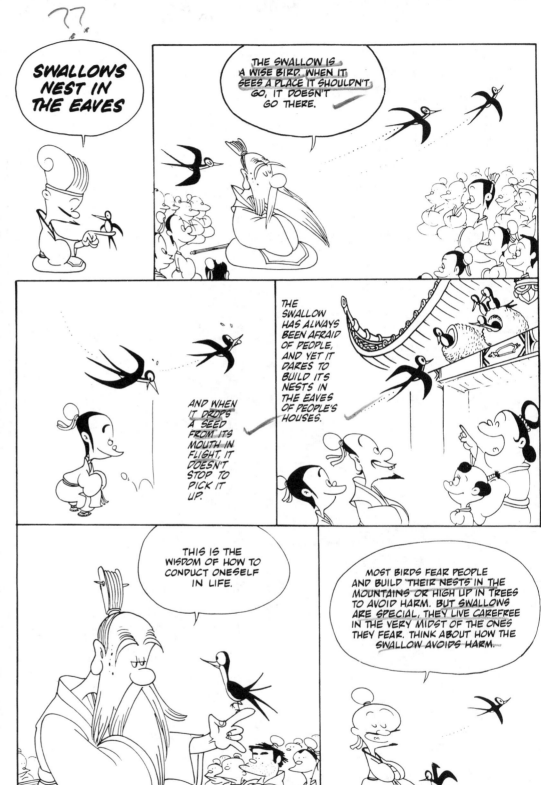

莊周遊於雕陵之樊，覩一異鵲自南方來者，翼廣七尺，目大運寸，感周之顙而集於栗林。莊周曰：「此何鳥哉，翼殷不逝，目大不覩？」蹇裳躩步，執彈而留之。覩一蟬，方得美蔭而忘其身；螳蜋執翳而搏之，見得而忘其形；異鵲從而利之，見利而

忘其真。莊周怵然曰：「噫！物固相累，二類相召也！」捐彈而反走，虞人逐而誶之。

莊周反入，三月不庭。藺且從而問之：「夫子何為頃間甚不庭乎？」莊周曰：「吾守形而忘身，觀於濁水而迷於清淵

83

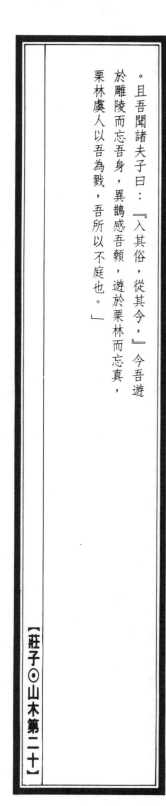

知北遊於玄水之上，登隱弅之丘，而適遭无為謂焉。知謂无為謂曰：「予欲有問乎若：何思何慮則知道？何處何服則安道？何從何道則得道？」三問而无為謂不答也，非不答，不知答也。

知不得問，反於白水之南，登狐闋之上，而睹狂屈焉。知以之言也問乎狂屈。狂屈曰：「唉！予知之，將語若，中欲言而忘其所欲言。」

知不得問，反於帝宮，見黃帝而問焉。黃帝曰：「无思无慮始知道，无處无服始安道，无從无道始

得道。」

知問黃帝曰：「我與若知之，彼與彼不知也，其孰是邪？」黃帝曰：「彼无為謂真是也，狂屈似之；我與汝終不近也。夫知者不言，言者不知，故聖人行不言之教。道不可致，德不可至。仁可為也，義可虧也，禮相偽也。故曰，『失道而後德，失德而後仁，失仁而後義，失義而後禮。禮者，道之華而亂之首也。』故曰，『為道者日損，損之又損之以至於无為，无為而无不為也。』今已為物也，欲復歸根，不亦難乎！其易也，其唯大人乎！

【莊子◎知北遊第二十二】

老聃之役有庚桑楚者，偏得老聃之道，以北居畏壘之山，其臣之畫然知者去之，其妾之挈然仁者遠之；擁腫之與居，鞅掌之為使。居三年，畏壘大壤。畏壘之民相與言曰：一庚桑子之始來，吾洒然異之，今吾日計之而不足，歲計之而有餘。庶幾其聖人乎！子胡不相與尸而祝之，社而稷之乎？」

庚桑子聞之，南面而不釋然。弟子異之。庚桑子曰：「弟子何異於予？夫春氣發而百草生，正得秋而萬寶成。夫春與秋，豈无得而然哉？天道已行矣。吾聞至人，尸居環堵之室，而百姓猖狂不知所如往。今以畏壘之細民而竊竊焉欲俎豆予于賢人之間，我其杓之人邪！吾是以不釋於老聃之言。」

【莊子◉庚桑楚第二十三】

GENGSANG FORSAKES FAME

GENGSANG OF CHU WAS A VERY ADEPT STUDENT OF LAOZI. ✓

WHILE HE WAS LIVING ON A CLIFF OVERLOOKING THE VILLAGE OF WEI LEI, HARVEST TIME CAME AROUND AND THE VILLAGERS HAD A BUMPER CROP. THEY ATTRIBUTED THEIR GOOD FORTUNE TO GENGSANG OVERSEEING THEM AND SO BEGAN TO WORSHIP AND GIVE THANKS TO HIM. GENGSANG SAID TO HIS DISCIPLES:

IN THE SPRINGTIME, LEAVES BEGIN TO GROW AND FLOWERS BLOSSOM.

IN THE LATE SUMMER, PLANTS COME TO FRUITION. IT'S THE COURSE OF NATURE! BUT PEOPLE SAY I AM RESPONSIBLE FOR IT JUST BECAUSE I LIVE UP HERE. THEY THINK I AM SOME KIND OF SAGE.

THEREUPON, GENGSANG MOVED AWAY TO THE FOREST.

教子曰：『若乘日之車而遊於襄城之野。』今予病少痊，予又且後遊於六合之外。夫為天下亦若此而已，予又奚事焉！」

黃帝曰：「夫為天下者，則誠非吾子之事。雖然，請問為天下。」小童辭。黃帝又問。小童曰：「

夫為天下者，亦奚以異乎牧馬者哉！亦去其害馬者而已矣！」

黃帝再拜稽首，稱天師而退。

THE STONE MASON AND THE YING MAN

AFTER HUIZI PASSED AWAY ZHUANGZI MISSED HIM VERY MUCH.

HUIZI R.I.P.

ONCE THERE WAS A CITIZEN OF THE CITY OF YING WHO WAS PATCHING UP A BUILDING WHEN A LITTLE BIT OF LIME AS THIN AS A FLY'S WING DRIPPED DOWN ON TO HIS NOSE.

HEY, CAN YOU HELP ME CHOP OFF THIS LITTLE BIT OF LIME?

READY?

READY!

THE MAN FROM YING STOOD STILL AS THE BLOW CAME, AND THE LIME WAS CUT AWAY WITHOUT THE SLIGHTEST HARM TO HIS NOSE.

PERFECT!

莊子送葬，過惠子之墓，顧謂從者曰：「郢人堊慢其鼻端若蠅翼，使匠石斲之。匠石運斤成風，聽而斲之，盡堊而鼻不傷，郢人立不失容。宋元君聞之，召匠石曰：『嘗試為寡人為之。』匠石曰：『臣則嘗能斲之。雖然，臣之質死久矣，吾无以為質矣，吾无與言之矣。」自夫子之死也，吾无以為質矣，吾无與言之矣。」

【莊子◎徐无鬼第二十四】

【莊子◎徐无鬼第二十四】

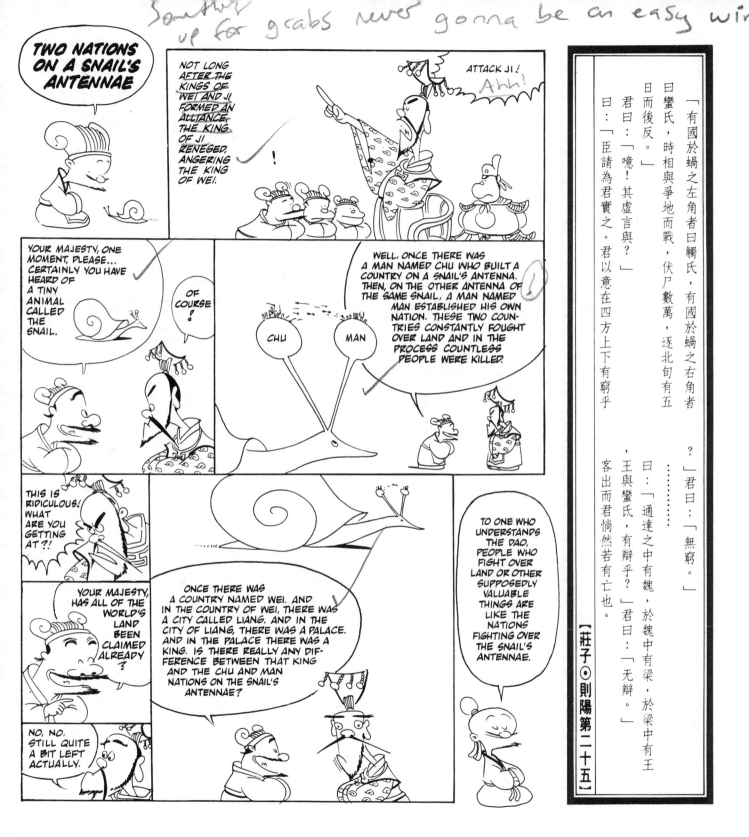

莊周家貧，故往貸粟於監河侯。監河侯曰：「諾。我將得邑金，將貸子三百金，可乎？」莊周忿然作色曰：「周昨來，有中道而呼者。周顧視車轍中，有鮒魚焉。周問之曰：『鮒魚來！子何為者邪？』對曰：『我，東海之波臣也。君豈有斗升之水而活我哉？』周曰：『諾。我且南遊吳越之王，激西江之水而迎子，可乎？』鮒魚忿然作色曰：『吾失我常與，我無所處。吾得斗升之水然活耳，君乃言此，曾不如早索我於枯魚之肆！』」

【莊子◎外物第二十六】

【莊子◉外物第二十六】

：一殺龜以卜吉。」乃刳龜，七十二鑽而無遺筴。

仲尼曰：「神龜能見夢於元君，而不能避余且之網；知能七十二鑽而無遺筴，不能避刳腸之患。如是，則知有所困，神有所不及也。雖有至知，萬人謀之。魚不畏網而畏鵜鶘。去小知而大知明，去善而自善矣。嬰兒生無石師而能言，與能言者處也。

Useful will rise

98

How to study the Dao

陽子居南之沛，老聃西遊於秦，邀於郊，至於梁而遇老子。老子中道仰天而歎曰：「始以汝為可教，今不可也。」

陽子居不答。至舍，進盥漱巾櫛，脱屨户外，膝行而前曰：「向者弟子欲請夫子，夫子行不閒，是以不敢，今閒矣，請問其過。」

老子曰：「而睢睢盱盱，而誰與居？大白若辱，盛德若不足。」

陽子居蹵然變容曰：「敬聞命矣！」

其往也，舍者迎將，其家公執席，妻執巾櫛，舍者避席，煬者避竈。其反也，舍者與之爭席矣。

【莊子⊙寓言第二十七】

ZI GONG'S SNOW-WHITE CLOTHES

YUAN XIAN AND ZI GONG WERE STUDENTS OF CONFUCIUS.

YUAN XIAN WAS VERY POOR. HE LIVED IN A HOUSE WHERE THE ROOF LEAKED...

...AND THERE WAS A BIG HOLE IN ONE OF THE WALLS. BUT HE DIDN'T MIND.

BEING A GOOD SPEAKER, ZI GONG BECAME A HIGH OFFICIAL AND WAS VERY PROUD OF HIMSELF. ONE DAY HE PAID A VISIT TO YUAN XIAN.

THE LANE IS TOO NARROW, SIR. THE CARRIAGE WON'T FIT.

原憲居魯，環堵之室，茨以生草，蓬戶不完，桑以為樞；而甕牖二室，褐以為塞；上漏下溼，匡坐而弦。

子貢乘大馬，中紺而表素，軒車不容巷，往見原憲。原憲華冠縰履，杖藜而應門。

子貢曰：「嘻！先生何病？」

原憲應之曰：「憲聞之，无財謂之貧，學而不能行謂之病。今憲，貧也，非病也。」

子貢逡巡而有愧色。

原憲笑曰：「夫希世而行，比周而友，學以為人

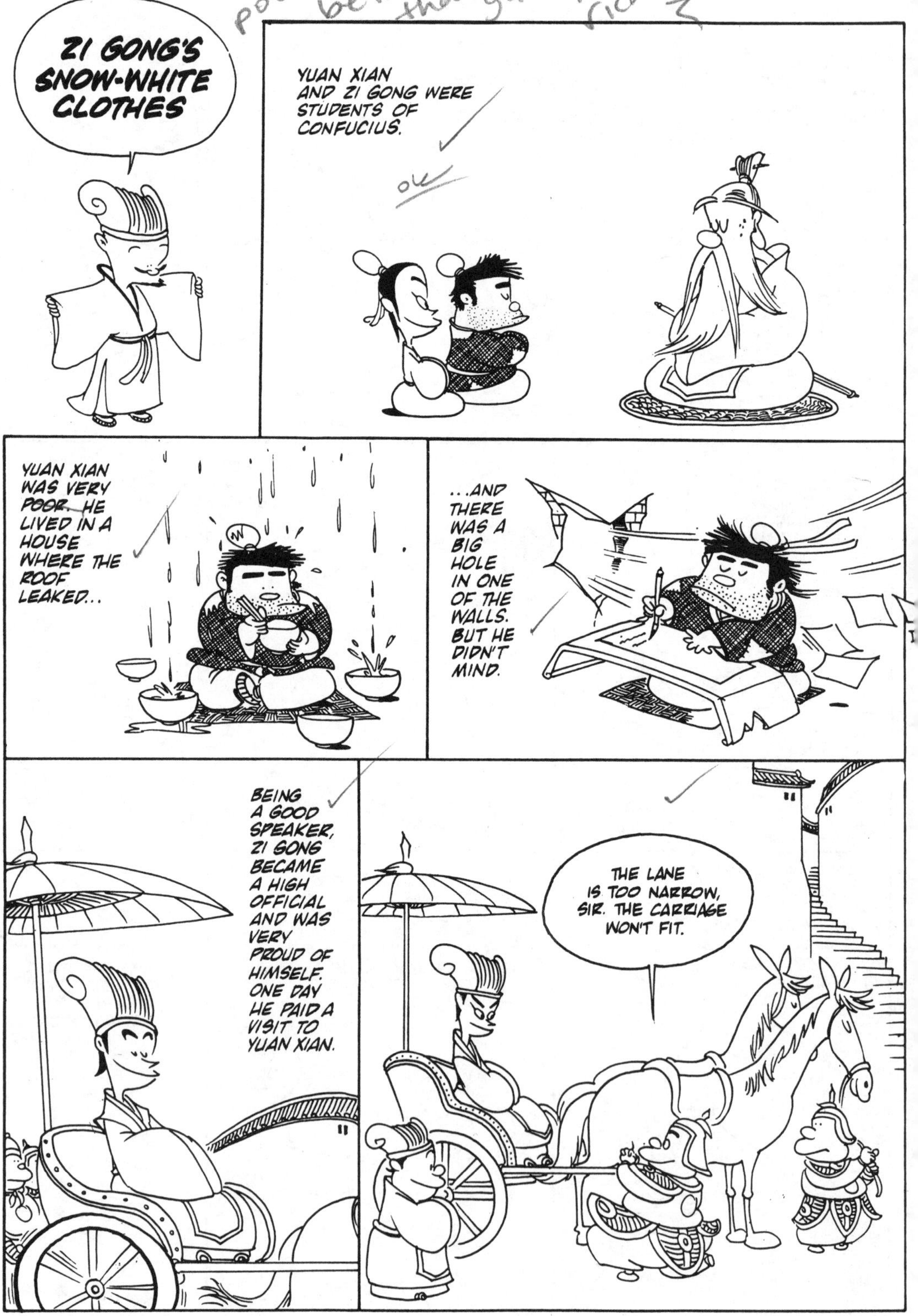

100

教以為己，仁義之慝，輿馬之飾，憲不忍為也。」

【莊子◎讓王第二十八】

101

孔子與柳下季為友，柳下季之弟，名曰盜跖。盜跖從卒九千人，橫行天下，侵暴諸侯，穴室樞戶，驅人牛馬，取人婦女，貪得忘親，不顧父母兄弟，不祭先祖。所過之邑，大國守城，小國入保，萬民苦之。

孔子謂柳下季曰：「夫為人父者，必能詔其子；為人兄者，必能教其弟。若父不能詔其子，兄不能教其弟，則无貴父子兄弟之親矣。今先生，世之才士也，弟為盜跖，為天下害，而弗能教也，丘竊為先生羞之。丘請為先生往說之。」

THE BANDIT SPEAKS

LIUXIA JI WAS A FRIEND OF CONFUCIUS AND HAD A LITTLE BROTHER KNOWN AS ZHI THE BANDIT. ZHI THE BANDIT HAD NINE THOUSAND FOLLOWERS AND TOGETHER THEY RAVAGED THE LAND.

PARENTS SHOULD TEACH THEIR CHILDREN AND OLDER BROTHERS SHOULD TEACH THEIR YOUNGER BROTHERS. YOUR LITTLE BROTHER IS A TERRIBLE VILLAIN AND RAVAGES THE LAND. ISN'T THERE ANYTHING YOU CAN DO?

WHAT CAN I DO? SOME PEOPLE JUST DON'T LISTEN.

WELL, THEN LET ME HAVE A TRY!

LOOK, MY BROTHER HAS A BAD TEMPER. IF YOU CROSS HIM, I CAN'T SAY WHAT MIGHT HAPPEN. I THINK IT WOULD BE BETTER IF YOU DIDN'T GO.

柳下季曰：「先生言為人父者必能詔其子，為人兄者必能教其弟，若子不聽父之詔，弟不受兄之教，雖今先生之辯、將柰之何哉！且跖之為人也，心如涌泉，意如飄風，強足以距敵，辯足以飾非，順其心則喜，逆其心則怒，易辱人以言。先生必无往。」

孔子不聽，顏回為馭，子貢為右，往見盜跖。盜跖乃方休卒徒大山之陽，膾人肝而餔之。孔子下車而前，見謁者曰：「魯人孔丘，聞將軍高義，敬再拜謁者。」

孔子曰：「丘聞之，凡天下有三德：生而長大，美好無雙，少長貴賤見而皆說之，此上德也；知維天地，能辯諸物，此中德也；勇悍果敢，聚眾率兵，此下德也。凡人有此一德者，足以南面稱孤矣。

今將軍兼此三者，身長八尺二寸，面目有光，脣如激丹，齒如齊貝，音中黃鍾，而名曰盜跖，丘竊為將軍恥不取焉。將軍有意聽臣，臣請南使吳越，北使齊魯，東使宋衛，西使晉楚，使為將軍造大城數百里，立數十萬戶之邑，尊將軍為諸侯，與天下更

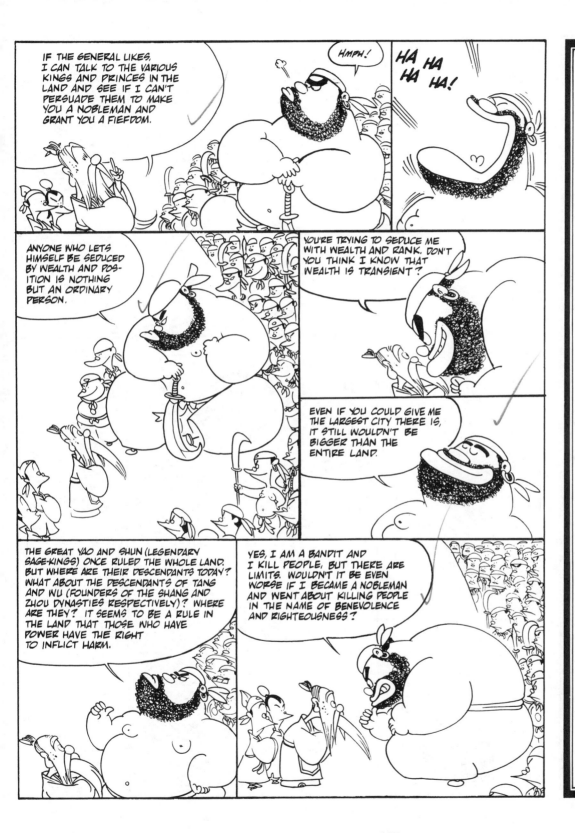

始，罷兵休卒，收養昆弟，共祭先祖。此聖人才士之行，而天下之願也。」

盜跖大怒曰：「丘來前！夫可規以利而可諫以言者，皆愚陋恆民之謂耳。今長大美好，人見而悅之者，此吾父母之遺德也。丘雖不吾譽，吾獨不自知邪？且吾聞之，好面譽人者，亦好背而毀之。今丘告我以大城眾民，是欲規我以利而恆民畜我也，安可久長也！城之大者，莫大乎天下矣。堯舜有天下，子孫无置錐之地；湯武立為天子，而後世絕滅；非以其利大故邪？

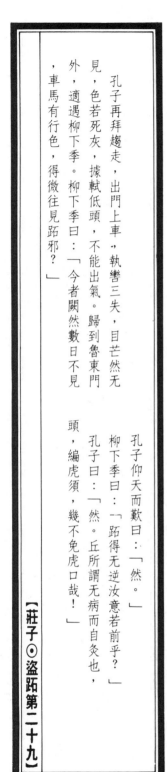

【莊子◎盜跖第二十九】

孔子再拜趨走，出門上車，執轡三失，目芒然無
見，色若死灰，據軾低頭，不能出氣。歸到魯東門
外，適遇柳下季。柳下季曰：「今者闕然數日不見
，車馬有行色，得微往見跖邪？」

孔子仰天而歎曰：「然。」

柳下季曰：「跖得無逆汝意若前乎？」

孔子曰：「然。丘所謂無病而自灸也，
頭，編虎須，幾不免虎口哉！」

昔趙文王喜劍，劍士夾門而客三千餘人，日夜相擊於前，死傷者歲百餘人，好之不厭。如是三年，國衰，諸侯謀之。

太子悝患之，募左右曰：「孰能說王之意止劍士者，賜之千金。」左右曰：「莊子當能。」

太子乃使人以千金奉莊子。莊子弗受，與使者俱，往見太子曰：「太子何以教周，賜周千金？」太子曰：「聞夫子明聖，謹奉千金以幣從者。夫子弗受，悝尚何敢言！」莊子曰：「聞太子所欲用周者，欲絕王之喜好也

。使臣上說大王而逆王意，下不當太子，則身刑而
死，周尚安所事金乎？使臣上說大王，下當太子，
趙國何求而不得也！」
太子曰：「然。吾王所見，唯劍士也。」
莊子曰：「諾。周善為劍。」

太子曰：「然吾王所見劍士，皆蓬頭突鬢垂冠，
曼胡之纓，短後之衣，瞋目而語難，王乃説之。今
夫子必儒服而見王，事必大逆。」
莊子曰：「請治劍服。」治劍服三日，乃見太子
太子乃與見王，王脱白刃待之。莊子入殿門不趨

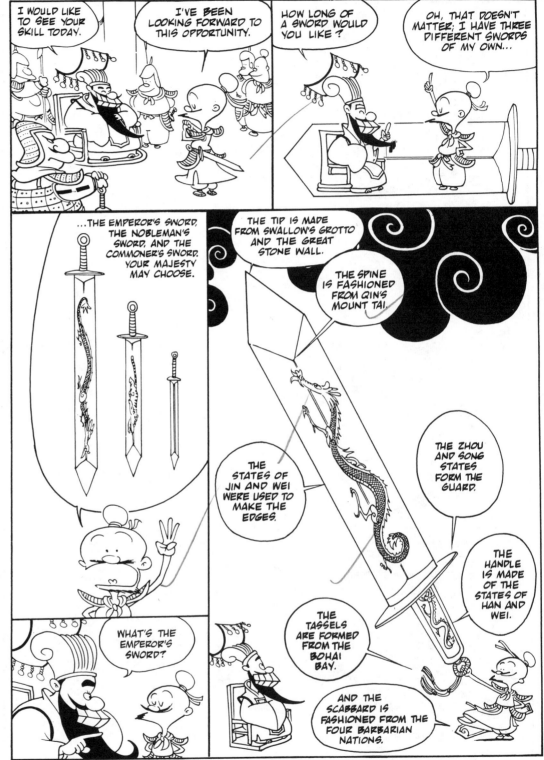

晉魏為脊，周宋為鐔，韓魏為夾；包以四夷，裹以四時；繞以渤海，帶以常山；制以五行，論以刑德；開以陰陽，持以春夏，行以秋冬。此劍，直之無前，舉之無上，案之無下，運之無旁，上決浮雲，下絕地紀。此劍一用，匡諸侯，天下服矣。此天子之劍也。」

文王芒然自失，曰：「諸侯之劍何如？」

曰：「諸侯之劍，以知勇士為鋒，以清廉士為鍔，以賢良士為脊，以忠聖士為鐔，以豪桀士為夾。此劍，直之亦無前，舉之亦無上，案之亦無下，運之亦无旁；上法圓天以順三光，下法方地以順四時，中和民意以安四鄉。此劍一用，如雷霆之震也，四封之內，無不賓服而聽從君命者矣。此諸侯之劍也。」

王曰：「庶人之劍何如？」

曰：「庶人之劍，蓬頭突鬢垂冠，曼胡之纓，短後之衣，瞋目而語難。相擊於前，上斬頸領，下決肝肺。此庶人之劍，无異於鬪雞，一旦命已絕矣，无所用於國事。今大王有天子之位而好庶人之劍，臣竊為大王薄之。」

王乃牽而上殿。宰人上食，王三環之。莊子曰：

「大王安坐定氣，劍事已畢奏矣。」

於是文王不出宮三月，劍士皆服斃其處也。

【莊子⊙說劍第三十】

113

孔子遊乎緇帷之林，休坐乎杏壇之上。弟子讀書，孔子絃歌鼓琴，奏曲未半。有漁父者，下船而來，須眉交白，被髮揄袂，行原以上，距陸而止，左手據膝，右手持頤以聽。曲終而招子貢子路，二人俱對。

客指孔子曰：「彼何為者也？」子路對曰：「魯之君子也。」客問其族。子路對曰：「族孔氏。」客曰：「孔氏者何治也？」子路未應，子貢對曰：「孔氏者，性服忠信，身

114

行仁義，飾禮樂，選人倫，上以忠於世主，下以化
於齊民，將以利天下。此孔氏之所治也。」

又問曰：「有土之君與？」
子貢曰：「非也。」
「侯王之佐與？」

子貢曰：「非也。」

孔子再拜而起曰：「丘少而脩學，以至於今，六
十九歲矣，无所得聞至教，敢不虛心！」

客曰：「……且人有八疵，事有四患，不可不察

115

也。非其事而事之，謂之摠；莫之顧而進之，謂之佞；希意道言，謂之諂；不擇是非而言，謂之諛；好言人之惡謂之讒；析交離親，謂之賊；稱譽詐偽以敗惡人，謂之慝；不擇善否，兩容頰適，偷拔其所欲，謂之險。此八疵者，外以亂人，內以傷身，

君子不友，明君不臣。所謂四患者：好經大事，變更易常，以挂功名，謂之叨；專知擅事，侵人自用，謂之貪；見過不更，聞諫愈甚，謂之很；人同於己則可，不同於己，雖善不善，謂之矜。此四患也。能去八疵，无行四患，而始可教已。

【莊子◎漁父第三十一】

人有畏影惡迹而去之走者；舉足愈數而迹愈多，走愈疾而影不離身，自以為尚遲，疾走不休，絕力而死。不知處陰以休影，處靜以息迹，愚亦甚矣！

【莊子◎漁父第三十一】

〔莊子◉漁父第三十一〕

人有畏影惡迹而去之走者，舉足愈數而迹愈多，走愈疾而影不離身，自以為尚遲，疾走不休，絕力而死。不知處陰以休影，處靜以息迹，愚亦甚矣！

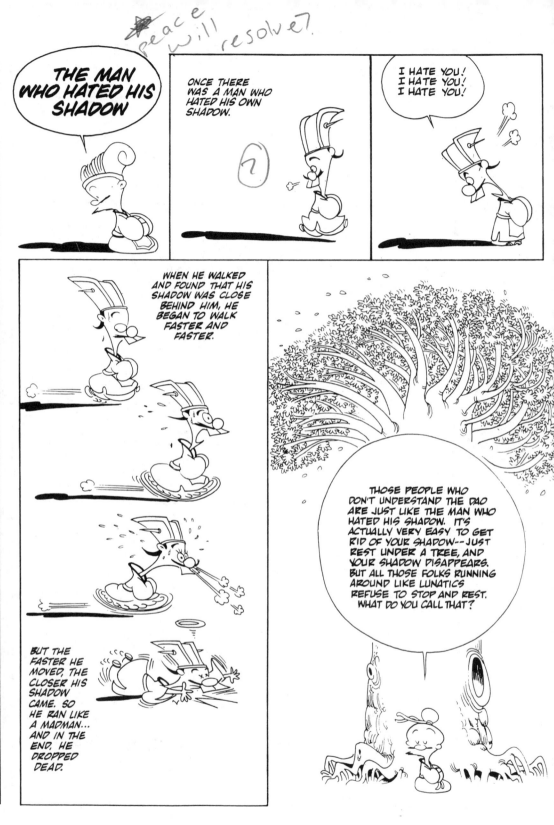

THE MAN WHO HATED HIS SHADOW

ONCE THERE WAS A MAN WHO HATED HIS OWN SHADOW.

I HATE YOU! I HATE YOU! I HATE YOU!

WHEN HE WALKED AND FOUND THAT HIS SHADOW WAS CLOSE BEHIND HIM, HE BEGAN TO WALK FASTER AND FASTER.

BUT THE FASTER HE MOVED, THE CLOSER HIS SHADOW CAME. SO HE RAN LIKE A MADMAN... AND IN THE END, HE DROPPED DEAD.

THOSE PEOPLE WHO DON'T UNDERSTAND THE DAO ARE JUST LIKE THE MAN WHO HATED HIS SHADOW. IT'S ACTUALLY VERY EASY TO GET RID OF YOUR SHADOW--JUST REST UNDER A TREE, AND YOUR SHADOW DISAPPEARS. BUT ALL THOSE FOLKS RUNNING AROUND LIKE LUNATICS REFUSE TO STOP AND REST. WHAT DO YOU CALL THAT?

LIKE A DRIFTING BOAT

people w/ knowledge still don't admit it

TALENTED PEOPLE HAVE SO MUCH WORK TO DO.

really?

INTELLIGENT PEOPLE HAVE SO MUCH TO WORRY ABOUT.

BUT INCOMPETENT PEOPLE GO ABOUT OH-SO-HAPPILY, SEEKING NOTHING AND SATISFIED WITH ENOUGH TO EAT.

...LIKE AN UNMOORED BOAT, DRIFTING ON THE WATER, ROCKING GENTLY BACK AND FORTH, CAREFREE AND AT EASE.

PEOPLE OF ABILITY AND INTELLIGENCE ALWAYS BRING ON SUFFERING AND DISTRESS, WHICH IS SOMETHING THE AVERAGE PERSON OFTEN DOESN'T REALIZE.

巧者勞而知者憂，无能者无所求，飽食而敖遊，汎若不繫之舟，虛而敖遊者也。

【莊子⊙列禦寇第三十二】

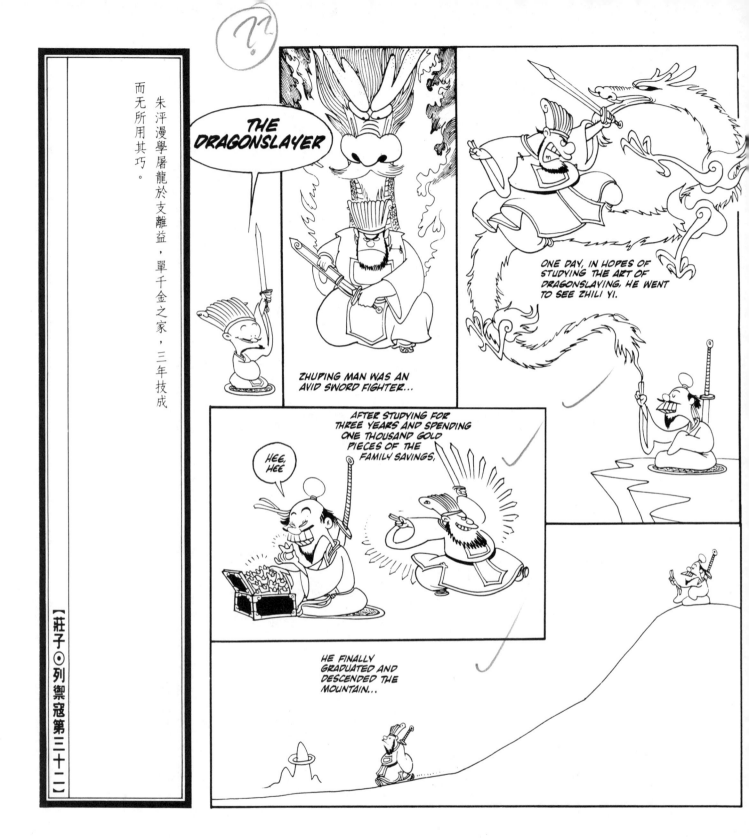

朱泙漫學屠龍於支離益，單千金之家，三年技成而无所用其巧。

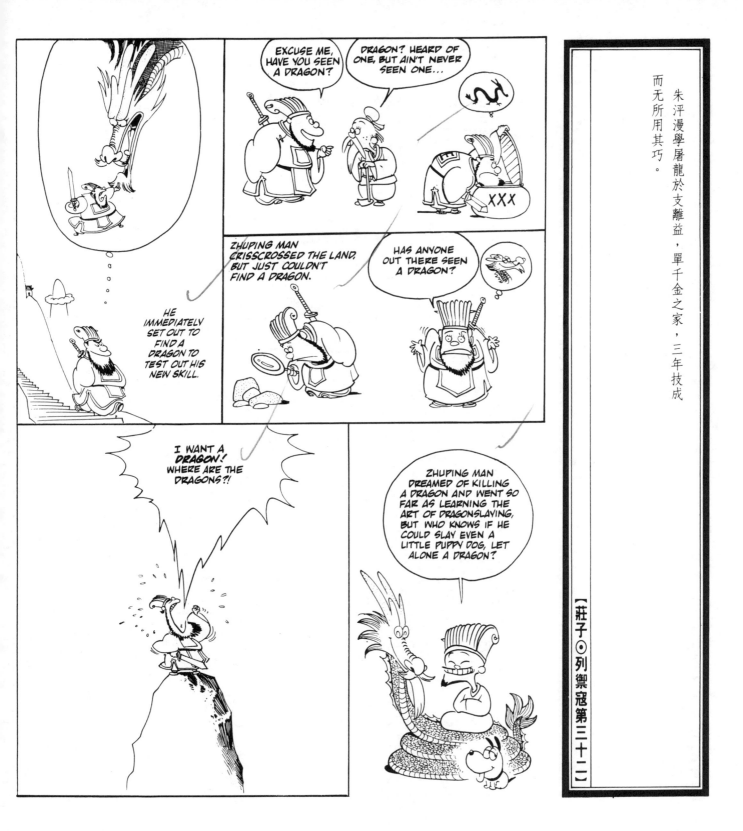

朱泙漫學屠龍於支離益，單千金之家，三年技成而无所用其巧。

【莊子◎列禦寇第三十二】

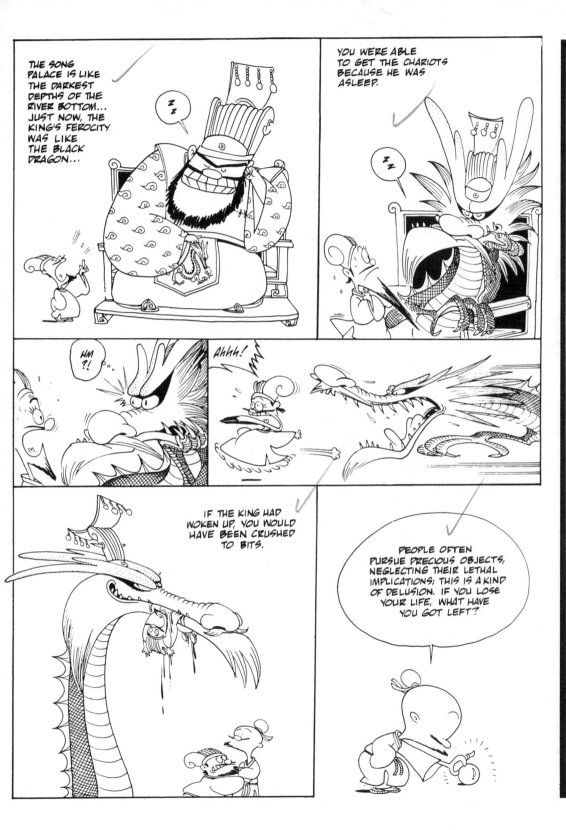

人有見宋王者，錫車十乘，以其十乘驕稚莊子。莊子曰：「河上有家貧恃緯蕭而食者，其子沒於淵，得千金之珠。其父謂其子曰：『取石來鍛之！夫千金之珠，必在九重之淵而驪龍頷下，子能得珠者，必遭其睡也。使驪龍而寤，子尚奚微之有哉！今宋國之深，非直九重之淵也；宋王之猛，非直驪龍也；子能得車者，必遭其睡也。使宋王而寤，子為韲粉夫！』」

【莊子⦿列禦寇第三十二】

123

125

AFTERWORD

Societies may well need rules, standards used to justify those rules, and officials to enforce them. It seems fairly obvious that such restrictions can help minimize some forms of disorder that threaten our tranquillity and survival. But too many rules, including rules of etiquette, constrain us, and make us feel suffocated. Our psyches seek out routes of escape. We find release in the mountains, in wine bottles, or in beliefs that undercut the significance of the suffocating rules and standards. This book is about Zhuangzi (369?–286? B.C.), a man who broke a lot of the rules and was irreverent toward all the rest.

Over the centuries, China's gentlemen scholars were educated with classical texts that primarily discussed such rules, standards, and the model officials who embodied them. They believed that those texts—those teachings—came from Confucius (551–479 B.C.) and his disciples. About eighteen centuries after Confucius, starting in 1313, four of the texts and commentaries to them formed the basis for the civil service examinations that constituted the path to privilege. The scholars and government servants considered themselves to be Confucians, or Ruists, as they are known in China, and yet many of them also sought routes of escape. They often simultaneously accepted some of the teachings of Zhuangzi, which inspire this volume. These teachings allow us to stand back and smile at the serious Confucian social rules, and our psyches are freed from their control over us. Although Zhuangzi himself had never heard the Chinese equivalent of our term "Daoist," his teachings, along with others, have been categorized as Daoist since the second century before Christ. Thus, many gentlemen scholars were Confucians and Daoists at the same time. The inconsistencies did not seem to bother them, for they often appealed to the psychological consequences of a belief in supporting it, rather than to its logical validity. It certainly is true that we believe lots of things on grounds other than rational argument.

One of my own tutors, with whom I studied the classics in Taiwan, considered himself to be a good Confucian. He also complained about the number of stifling rules of etiquette that had been instilled in him as a youth—so many, for example, that he tried to avoid having to get up to go to the bathroom in the middle of the night because of all the rules about proper robes and belts and things hanging from belts that he had to observe. With that complaint, he would pass approvingly to some point of Zhuangzi. (He was not only an erudite Confucian classicist, who had also accepted many Daoist teachings, but a Buddhist as well!)

Confucianism and Daoism complement each other in additional ways. If Confucian learning hones an individual's respect for proper interpersonal relations, Daoism teaches proper respect for other living things. The Dao, as we shall see, is equally present in all of us.

There was no Daoist "school" when Zhuangzi lived. Our term Daoism is a translation of one of three expressions introduced in the second century B.C. to denote such a school: *daojia* (school of the Dao), *daodejia* (school of the Dao and *de*, which is the Dao in a thing), and *Huang-Lao* (the teachings that revered the Yellow Emperor and Laozi). When these designations came into use, two of the principal texts attributed to such schools were the *Zhuangzi* and the *Laozi*. No one knows who wrote the latter text, the first record of which is around 250 B.C. Most scholars believe that Zhuangzi himself was the author of the first seven chapters in the book that bears his name, and that later followers with differing perspectives wrote the other chapters. *Zhuangzi Speaks* draws mainly from those seven original or "inner" chapters.

Two differences between these Daoist texts are worth noting. The *Laozi* treats politics seriously, whereas the *Zhuangzi* inner chapters reveal almost no interest in politics or ruling. The texts also differ in the relative emphasis each places on the various traits of the Dao. The *Laozi* leans toward treat-ing it as the indivisible stuff from which all emerges, an "uncarved block," as the text says. It refers to the Dao as the Mother, which makes it easy for the reader to infer the Dao's temporal priority over the myriad individual things that stem from it. The *Zhuangzi* tends to explain the Dao as either the patterns of orderly change in nature or as the cause of those patterns. It is "the maker and transformer." The two books agree that the Dao is unitary. Its individuated presence in things is *de*, sometimes thought of as power or as a life principle. As the *Laozi* says, "Tao [Dao] produced them (the ten thousand things). Virtue [*de*] fosters them."[1]

The person who accepts the unity of the Dao avoids regarding things exclusively in terms of their transitory physical forms, because to do so is to consider what separates one thing from another rather than to think of their shared participation in the Dao. He or she also avoids taking seriously or being controlled by the words that people use to classify or categorize things. Language reinforces the tendency to treat things as discrete units rather than as parts of a unity. By avoiding these pitfalls and instead going spontaneously where the Dao leads, the individual will find that his *de* is enhanced.

Zhuangzi's followers past and present differ from other people in some basic ways. They do not think much of language as a key to unlocking nature's secrets, nor do they think much of the evaluative standards that language often communicates when a person passes judgment on something. They think about the nature of nature and how to live a life modeled on nature rather than a life governed by the moral rules written up in books.

A F T E R W O R D

Places and Ideas in the Background

Initially somewhat unified around 1122 B.C. under the Zhou dynasty, the territory sometimes known as China Proper was fragmented into a number of increasingly independent states after 771 B.C. These states and successors produced by increasingly violent interstate warfare were agricultural, not maritime, communities. Cut off from other civilizations by mountains and deserts to the north and west, and with only a small ocean perimeter to the east, they were self-contained units. Though culturally advanced, their lords and aristocratic retainers rarely had to submit their ritualized customs and the ideas on which they rested to competition from those of other strong and equally developed societies. The competition came from non-Chinese nomadic peoples in the north whose equestrian skills helped to make them a constant threat, and from peoples in the south who were also Chinese but culturally somewhat different.

Several of these states figure in the text *Zhuangzi*, which is so charmingly transformed in the drawings, conversational balloons, and translations of *Zhuangzi Speaks*. These include some of the states that once made up the old Zhou kingdom. One of these was Song (pp. 38, 92, 95). Another was Lu (p. 52), birthplace of Confucius, who belonged to an impoverished branch of its aristocracy. The Lu aristocracy prided itself on perpetuating the rituals and rules of the early Zhou. Jin, once the largest state of all, was fragmented around 403 because of internal bickering among its lords. Its fracture into the three smaller states of Han, Wei, and Zhao (pp. 107, 110) signaled the beginning of the aptly named Warring States Period.

As our text relates on p. 105, villains ravaged the land. When Zhao finally succumbed, the records report that 400,000 of its soldiers were buried alive.

Outside of these core states were two others that figure in this harsh scene. Both were Chinese, but their customs were regarded as different and crude by the elites of the core states. The first, Chu, gradually expanded into the entire Yangtze valley. In 597 B.C. its soldiers, dressed in armor made of sharkskin and rhinoceros hide, routed the core states. The other fringe state was the northwestern state of Qin. It began an eastern expansion in 341 B.C. when it conquered the state of Wei, causing its ruler to flee to the eastern part of his state, to the the city of Liang mentioned on p. 93. This occurred during the lifetime of Zhuangzi, who was born around 369 B.C. Qin eventually conquered all of the other states, creating the first unified Chinese empire in 221 B.C.

Our cast of characters begins with Zhuangzi himself. He was a native of Song, though some say that his doctrines show more of the influence of Chu in the south. He enjoyed lively debates with his friend Hui Shi (p. 92), at one time the prime minister of Wei. Hui Shi opposed aggressive warfare, promoted a doctrine of universal love, and left behind some paradoxes ("The heavens are as low as the earth; mountains are on the same level as the marshes").[2] Famous for his rhetorical skills (p. 28), he shared with Zhuangzi a concern with distinctions between the various levels of meaning in words and was interested in the question of the standards according to which we make distinctions. Learning from him, Zhuangzi went beyond him to the treacherous point where the making of any distinctions potentially confounds us.

Among those considered by Zhuangzi to be obsessed with making distinctions were the Mohists and the Confucians. Taking as their patriarch the philosopher Mozi (c. 479–c. 381 B.C.), the Mohists employed a standard for the acceptability of beliefs that centered on a distinction between the useful and the useless, or that which benefits or does not benefit the people. Benefit might have been defined in terms of increasing wealth, social order, and cooperation without strife.

The Confucians, diverse in doctrinal details, worried about the distinction between ritually proper and improper behavior. Disciples of Confucius codified and transmitted orally extensive rules covering almost every aspect of interpersonal conduct, with particular attention to such activities as funerals and coming-of-age ceremonies. The criteria for determining propriety were, fundamentally, social role relationships (father-son, husband-wife, older brother–younger brother, prince-minister, friend-friend) and hierarchy. An individual's very identity was defined in relational terms (as father, husband, minister). Propriety varied as a function of role and hierarchical status. In the modern West we generally think of duties as universal. That is, if something is the right thing for you to do in a certain setting, it is the right thing for everyone everywhere to do in that circumstance. These Confucians, in contrast, treated duties as different for different people in the same setting, as a function of their different social roles or relationships. In a certain situation, I have duties to those with whom I have special relationships, and these are different from the duties that I would have to others in another situation, even when the factual conditions in the two cases are

otherwise identical. If I find that my father has stolen a sheep, I have a duty to protect him. If I find someone else with a stolen sheep, my duty may be to the sheep's rightful owner or to the laws of the state.

Confucian teachings also centered on the difference between humane or benevolent and nonbenevolent conduct. The possibility of a person's benevolence rests in his or her ability to nurture the kinship-love with which all humans are born, and to extend it to other people beyond the family. Benevolence manifests itself in an inability to tolerate suffering and, closer to home, in parental love and in children's filial piety toward their parents. Confucians, then, were known for their standard of ritualized propriety (based on relational roles and hierarchical status), infused with a sense of righteousness, and for their standard of benevolence. Hence on p. 114 someone describes Confucius as being a gentleman from Lu who "teaches people about benevolence and righteousness. . . . His sincere teachings convert the masses to goodness and bring peace to the whole land." This news brings the reply that "If he keeps on like this, he'll only grow farther and farther from the Dao!"

Like the Mohists, the Confucians sought employment at the courts of the lords who ruled the states. If the attitudes of Zhuangzi's contemporary, the orthodox Confucian Mencius (372?–289? B.C.) can be taken as typical, they were heavily judgmental of the moral failings of the rulers with whom they spoke. They criticized the rulers for not being benevolent, or for ignoring propriety, or for not consulting their inner moral sense. Although Mencius does not appear in the *Zhuangzi* chapters authored by Zhuangzi himself, it is worth noting the way in which he argued for his doctrines. Zhuangzi would have had plenty of oppor-

A F T E R W O R D

tunity to see the Confucians in action, as they debated with thinkers from competing schools such as Mohists, language philosophers like Hui Shi, and advocates of self-preservation as the only moral standard (Yang Zhu, mentioned on p. 99, is an example).

Mencius argued that humans are universally born with such traits as a sense of compassion and a sense of righteousness similar to what we call a conscience. In making this case, and in rebutting opponents, he typically relied on one or more of four types of argument: presenting empirical claims; appealing to a doctrine's psychological impact on people who accept it; using analogy; and appealing to the authority of various sage kings and administors.

Zhuangzi's approach, relying on parables, anecdotes, and flights of fantasy sets him apart from such styles of argument. He had little use for language as a tool for gaining access to knowledge. Instead, he used it with great skill to sensitize the reader to the instability of the standards that all debaters invoke to justify their arguments and the meanings that they assign to words. Like Socratic teachers, Zhuangzi used words to point the reader in the right direction rather than to indoctrinate. So parables and tales of the imagination served instead of assertions, claims, and arguments. He used these techniques also to depict the weakness of language as a vehicle for understanding the true nature of the world. This weakness centers on the boundaries that language carves artificially into nature. A prime culprit is the dualistic categories in which humans often express themselves, such as beautiful/ugly. The values that such words carry are only those of the speaker or of his school of thought, not ones that correspond to any standard present in nature. One style of Zhuangzi's

teaching was especially suited to drive home this point about the mismatch between language and reality: his droll way of putting into the mouths of Confucians positions that are just the reverse of what they were known to advocate. Confucius's favorite disciple, for example, learns "to forget benevolence and righteousness."

Although the Yellow Emperor appears in *Zhuangzi Speaks* (p. 87), as does Laozi ("Old Master"), neither appears in the sections of the *Zhuangzi* that were written by the historical Zhuangzi but only in chapters written by later followers, who adopted the "Huang-Lao" teachings that became popular in the late Warring States Period. "Huang-Lao," a former Han dynasty (206 B.C.–A.D. 35) expression, combines part of the Chinese name of the Yellow (*huang*) Emperor and part of the Old (*lao*) Master's name. The Huang-Lao followers revered Laozi and Zhuangzi as sages who had insight into the nature of the Dao or the principles of change according to which the world works. Whereas the original writings of Zhuangzi show no ecumenical interest and are unequivocally anti-Confucian and anti-Mohist, the Huang-Lao writings attempted to synthesize ideas from several schools. As the Han historian Sima Tan (d. 110 B.C.) put it, "they selected the good parts of Confucianism and Mohism and gathered the essentials of the School of Names and Legalists." And where the chapters authored by the historical Zhuangzi reveal no political interest, those of the Huang-Lao school advocate nonaction by rulers and zealous action by ministers.

Now that we know a little about the places and characters that figure in our work, it is time to turn to the music of nature and other matters that Zhuangzi richly illuminated.

A F T E R W O R D

"The Music of Nature"

Language. Technically speaking the music of nature is the spontaneous functioning of things, but more loosely it is also the wind (p. 17) and the sound of man-made instruments. Nature is free of emotions and the values that are conveyed in them. So, too, is the earth's music or the wind free of them. In addition, as the wind blows through all varieties of canyons and other formations on earth, it makes every conceivable sound. When people speak, they are simply more canyons through which wind blows. They may add emotion, evaluation, and meaning to the wind that emerges from their voice boxes, but it is just like the wind in the canyon. The evaluations, the emotions, are nothing once the wind has left the individual's mouth. Angus Graham, the leading Western interpreter of the *Zhuangzi*, has noted that Zhuangzi was thinking especially of the arguments made by thinkers of different schools in their debates or preaching. Their arguments are the "pipes of heaven," not different from the musical sounds made by the wind blowing through differently shaped hollows.

Zhuangzi's first target, then, was the debates themselves. Some debates involved assumptions that certain things are similar to each other and therefore different from all other things. Mencius was busy arguing, for instance, that all humans are similar in that they possess four psychological traits. As a result, he claimed, they are not only different from other animals but better. Others argued about whether a white horse is a horse, because a horse that is white is no longer just a 'horse'. The very words that they used in their debates, such as similarity, difference, horse, and white have no permanent meanings. They have only that which the debaters paste on them for the moment. These words have no enduring relation to anything in nature. They are just more music of nature.

What Zhuangzi was rejecting as futile was not simply verbal argumentation but also the distinctions on which it is based. His progress toward this insight was probably eased, ironically, by what he learned from his own intellectual sparring partner, Hui Shi. Zhuangzi learned from Hui's paradoxes that all of our spatial and temporal distinctions are relative to the perspective of the person making them. That is one of the points of Hui Shi's statement that the mountains are on the same level as the marshes. So they are, from the standpoint of the bird in flight. Hui made the same point when he said, "The sun at noon is the sun declining; the creature born is the creature dying."[3] The fate of the sun and of every creature born is to be part of a process of change with a beginning and an end. From the standpoint of the end, each is already on its way there an instant after noon or after birth. From the standpoint of today's actuarial specialist in an insurance office, a baby is already a statistic in terms of its progress toward death.

As Graham pointed out, Zhuangzi went beyond Hui Shi to maintain that all distinctions that humans make with language depend on the perspective or standard of the viewer or speaker. In part this was a message directed at the debaters and preachers, but it was also directed at all humans. Not only were the Confucians or the Mohists narrow-minded but so also was the person who thought that the perspective of his or her species accurately portrays reality. This is the significance of the exchange (pp. 65–67) between the frog, who thinks that the well where he lives is incredibly large, and the tortoise, who had crawled up from the ocean. The only body of water known to the frog was the well, and he naively used it as his standard of big and small. The tortoise knew the size of the Eastern Sea. He had a rather different standard.

Thus, although one audience for many of the critiques of dualistic distinctions may be people associated with certain schools of thought, the broader audience includes every person. Zhuangzi loved to tweak his readers about the distinction between the useful and the useless. He may have offended Mohist utilitarians in particular with this assault, but he simultaneously challenged widespread standards of what is useful. The "useless" *shu* tree is a good example. Its trunk is all lumps and bumps, and it curves this way and that. Most people would say that a tree, to be useful, would provide material for houses, food, and other items involved in *human* survival. In the carpenter's perspective, only straight trees are useful because they produce planks that align nicely with the plumb line. But the useless *shu* tree lived on and on. No logger cut it down, so the "useless" tree lived longer than the useful ones. This is one of many times when we encounter Zhuangzi's own hidden standards. One is to prize all things equally in which the Dao is present. So the tree's interest in staying out of harm's way counts for as much as the carpenter's interest in turning it into a roof. Further, if the carpenter will simply broaden his standard of the useful, he will discover that he can use the gnarled old tree after all, for shade during his afternoon snooze. But just when readers thought that they finally had an insight into what "useful" really is, Zhuangzi

nudged them to another insight (pp. 77–78): it is best not to think in terms of useful and useless at all, but rather to transcend these categories.

Language reflects one's arbitrarily selected standards of worth, according to Zhuangzi. "Although a duck's legs are very short, it certainly wouldn't want them lengthened," we learn on p. 48. Similarly, moralists categorize people as good (following the sagely way) or as evil. But moral standards can also be used to justify great harm. Almost any teaching can be used for a variety of ends. So, when on p. 51, someone suggests that "principles do more harm than good," the message is directed both to the Confucian moralist and to his popular audience.

Analysis and dualistic verbal categories generally go hand in hand. Among the problems with them is the damage they can do. The moralist provides the tyrant with justifications for his acts. The false sense that analysis provides us with an understanding of objective reality motivates humans to tamper with that reality accordingly. They think that, having figured out the laws of nature or read up on them in books, they can intrude into the process of life from birth to death, or into the way in which rivers spontaneously flow, with their dams and ditches. On p. 53 a wise and enlightened master tells us the result: "You say you want to use the vitality of the Dao to enhance the natural processes? This will only destroy them. Don't you understand that to use our intellect to change things only makes matters worse?" The problem is not simply that the Confucian or Mohist is fooled into thinking that he is saying something about reality. It is also that he is stimulated by such evaluation to desire or try to possess the object categorized in a certain way, and this leads to conflict with other persons. Further, such language categories inhibit individuals from both experiencing nonverbally the whole and from treating things in the world in a manner that reflects this sense of harmony. The following concludes an exchange between three delightfully named persons on p. 87: "The man named Knowledge was of the realm of words, while Absurd was of the realm of language without words, and Can't Say was of the realm of no mind, no words. The Dao cannot be understood through words alone."

Skills. There are alternatives to manipulating words; one is practicing a skill in the manner of a master craftsman. The clue to this fact lies in Zhuangzi's exemplary models, people such as the skilled cook (p. 29). He does not consult a textbook on butchery but intuitively moves about the skeletal structure of the cow. "You see, when I butcher a cow, it's not skill that I use. It's the Dao," he says. He continues by describing the difference between his knife and that of the average cook: "The average cook goes through a knife every month, because he hacks and chops. . . . Because I neither hack nor chop, I've used this same knife for nineteen years, and it's still like new." There is an elderly wheelwright who appears on pp. 55–56, making the point that skills cannot be passed on through books. Sages may have had skills, but the words attributed to them in books are "merely the dregs of a dead man." The words are traces, shadows, having nothing of substance in common with those who left them behind. The wheelwright was unable to pass his skill on to his own son.

To practice a skill in the manner of a master is not to grasp the Dao, but it is to grasp one aspect of the Dao. It is to understand how to accord with natural patterns in cows or pieces of wood as one

applies a knife or chisel. There are many different skills, so a comprehensive understanding of the Dao is probably beyond the scope of what most people can hope for. It is a prize for the perfect person.

There is something in the traits of Zhuangzi's skilled craftsmen that was shared by the Confucian sage. This is action that is perfectly appropriate for the circumstances, though it emerges without analysis of the situation or planning. The *Analects* of Confucius was compiled in the early Warring States Period; it is an edited text of sayings and conversations of Confucius with disciples and others, compiled on the basis of records made by disciples and their disciples, or later Confucians who thought they knew what the Master would have said. It includes a statement by Confucius depicting his long progress to the most desirable condition, one that he attained only at the age of seventy. Confucius described the condition as one in which his desires and the dictates of the ritual rules of conduct were entirely convergent. The right thing to do and what he desires to do are the same. Only years of training in the practice of the rules can produce this result, a process that social scientists today would call socialization. But this state is one in which proper conduct for each situation is effortless. Moral acts are spontaneous. Spontaneity is the trait shared by the dexterous cook and by the elderly Confucius.

Unlike their counterparts in classical Greece (the Golden Age of which lasted from 461 to 431 B.C.), these Chinese thinkers did not portray the highest form of self-development as an ability to use reason. For those Greeks, reason was used either to deduce what principle to follow or, practically, how to implement it. For our Chinese figures, however, human cognitive functions need play no direct role in the sage's actions. Thoughtlessness, not thought, was prized. But there remains a crucial difference between the spontaneity advocated by Confucius and by Zhuangzi. Confucian spontaneity is always goal-directed. A person practices the ritual forms of conduct for the purpose, most immediately, of having all acts conform to the moral rules; more distantly, for the goal of becoming a morally superior person; and ultimately, to transform all the world into a Confucian moral utopia. An attitude of commitment to these goals informs every spontaneous act, as a person effortlessly does the right thing. Psychologically it is a powerfully practical response to the alienation that people might feel when there is a gap between what they want to do and what somebody tells them to do.

Having rejected both verbal rules and moral hierarchies, Zhuangzi prized spontaneity of a different kind: the ability to adapt immediately to whatever circumstance presents itself. Spontaneity is also found in skill mastery. Some of Zhuangzi's favorite examples of the former concern the acceptance of death:

Suddenly Master Lai grew ill. Gasping and wheezing, he lay at the point of death. His wife and children gathered round in a circle and began to cry. Master Li, who had come to ask how he was, said, "Shoo! Get back! Don't disturb the process of change!"

Then he leaned against the doorway and talked to Master Lai. "How marvelous the Creator Dao is! What is he going to make out of you next? Where is he going to send you? Will he make you into a rat's liver? Will he make you into a bug's arm?"

Master Lai said, "A child, obeying his father and mother, goes wherever he is told, east or west, south or north." And the yin and yang—how much more are they to a man than father or mother! Now that they have brought me to the verge of death, if I should refuse to obey them, how perverse I would be![4]

Spontaneity. The spontaneously adaptive response is characteristic of the person in whom the True Ruler of the body is not the evaluating or knowing mind, but the Dao itself. Such a person flows with nature's changes, as the Ruler turns his mind into a mirror. "The Perfect Man uses his mind like a mirror—going after nothing, welcoming nothing, responding but not storing."[5] The mirror suggests both immediate responsiveness to any circumstance and the absence of evaluation; the mirror reflects everything, what humans may call the beautiful and the ugly alike. Our present text has an episode in which Confucius went to see Laozi. He reported that he "saw a dragon, flowing with the Yin and Yang, ceaselessly changing" (p. 59). Although the chapters in the *Zhuangzi* text by Zhuangzi himself do not refer to Laozi, this characterization fits Zhuangzi's model of a person with the mirrorlike mind.

Angus Graham has written convincingly that to mirror things means "to face facts" and to "deal with things the way they objectively are, not as one would like them to be."[6] This means that Zhuangzi was not advocating that the individual become simply a passive respondent with no contribution to a given situation. Rather, the mirror mind is one devoid of prejudicial attachment to the dogmas of any particular school or way of thinking. Those prejudices would interfere with the ability to grasp the objective facts and respond as those facts demand. Attaining such a state takes considerable practice in "forgetting" the standards and language habits with which a person is daily socialized. To have a mirror mind is to have a clear mind, clear about the objective situation and swept clean of previous ideas that would impede the absorption of new facts.

Nature and the Dao. To flow with the changes, as Laozi was said to have done, is to avoid the purposeful pursuit of goods or goals evaluated as more worthy than other things. To be this way is to emulate a trait of Heaven (nature) and the Dao. Both are devoid of purpose or any differences of value. Herein lies a fascinating tale of how Zhuangzi's ideas fit in with other developments in China before and shortly after he lived.

The term Dao in the *Zhuangzi* has several meanings. One refers to that which simultaneously causes the ceaseless changes in nature and also somehow integrates or unifies all things that participate in those changes. Zhuangzi used the expression "maker and transformer" to convey this point. There is another meaning that the outside analyst can distinguish as separate from the one just given, though it would not have been separated by Zhuangzi. That is the orderly process or pattern of change itself. This meaning is present when our current text encourages us on p. 47 to "follow the laws of nature, or the Dao." This is also "flowing with the Yin and Yang" (p. 59). In neither of these two senses is the Dao purposive. To attribute purpose to the Dao is to give it a human trait, and that Zhuangzi did not do.

The Confucians, however, did. As early as the *Analects* there is reference to the fact that the pole star, being superior, receives obedience from the other stars, which are inferior to it. There is a statement in the *Mencius* that Heaven has the property of integrity or being true to itself. This property suggests that all natural processes are disposed to complete themselves, or it may mean that something possesses all of the qualities of which it is capable, or is fully in accord with its nature. Xunzi (c. 310–c. 210 B.C.), a Confucian who was born near the end of Zhuangzi's life, developed a full-fledged teleological view of nature. That is, he claimed that nature exhibits not simply order but order with a purpose. Things were described by him as either incomplete, on their way to completion, or complete. The collective purpose of things, he held, is the avoidance of chaos and the maintenance of hierarchy and proper relations between things. Heaven is high in status, earth is lower. Chaos is avoided when things keep to their places and fulfill their natural courses of development. The language was similar to the Aristotelian teleology that dominated medieval Europe. "Each thing should gain its proper place," and the condition to prize was "completeness," as Xunzi put it. He said that humans can avoid chaos by taking Heaven as a model through the establishment of hierarchically ranked social-role distinctions and by ensuring that people take as their individual goals the fulfillment of role duties.

In contrast to the Confucians, Zhuangzi was remarkable in refusing to attribute any of these human traits to the Dao (the patterns of change). It was, he held, devoid of purpose. Zhuangzi's view of nature also opposed that of Mozi, who taught that Heaven was an anthropomorphic deity who willed sanctions to reward and punish people according to whether they followed or disobeyed principles of universal love and utility.

The historical significance of Zhuangzi's view of nature is apparent when we realize that in the West it was not until the sixteenth and seventeenth centuries that people such as Copernicus and Descartes began to wipe nature clean of these human traits. In rejecting the geocentric view of

AFTERWORD

the universe, Copernicus laid the groundwork for others to eliminate both purposes and morally proper places from the natural and the social worlds. Descartes' God became the creator of matter and the giver of laws of motion, not a designer who built purpose into nature. For Descartes, nature has only quantitative characteristics.

In addition to reading human moral traits into nature, the Confucians, inspired by a position that appears in the *Analects*, rejected any division between what today would be called the secular and the sacred realms. As I am using the term, the sacred refers to things that are worthy of reverence, especially things such as rules that help produce order; it does not necessarily refer to the supernatural or to the religious. In terms of the objective world of nature, this meant that Confucian claims about order in nature both describe how regular changes such as seasonal cycles do in fact occur, and also state prescriptively how they should occur. The latter would detail the good patterns in nature worthy of our reverence. In terms of the human inner or psychological world, this meant that they taught that a person should remain mindful of moral standards in every act that he or she initiates. This includes guiding all acts with ritual rules, though the acts might be as different as acquiring knowledge and sweeping the floor. The *Analects* reports Confucius as saying, "Do not look at what is contrary to propriety, do not listen to what is contrary to propriety, do not speak what is contrary to propriety, and do not make any movement which is contrary to propriety."[7] In time, Confucians would maintain that the successful attainment of the purpose of any act depends on its agent being mindful of such a standard when the act was performed. Thus there was no secular study of nature's laws and no secular

realm of action. Zhuangzi, in contrast, not only stripped nature of traits derived from human morality, but also counseled human minds to forget rules and just adapt to the objective condition as it is. In a nutshell, in opposing the Confucian transformation of everything into the sacred, Zhuangzi advocated total secularization.

The Natural as a Model. Among the ideas shared by Zhuangzi and his Confucian opponents was the importance of models and the imitation of appropriate exemplars. Some of his models are those skilled craftsmen who spontaneously, without reference to textbooks, use their bodies in a way that is consistent with the requirements of the materials they use, and so make the movements necessary to their craft. The skilled cook is an example. Other models, such as Toeless Shu (p. 43) and the Freak (p. 40) are just the opposites of those examples of human perfection that were idealized by the Greeks, such as Adonis and Venus. One who does not put in an appearance in the present text is Mr. Lame-Hunchback-No-Lips. Obviously, Zhuangzi was making a statement about the unimportance of transitory human form when, in a moment of cosmic time, the stuff of which we are made will decompose and perhaps reappear as rats' livers. If these freaks are to be our models, we clearly should not copy customary ideas about physical beauty. Instead, we are to emulate the wisdom of these models.

The greatest model of all for Confucians, Mohists, and Zhuangzi was Heaven itself. Confucians were likely to advocate that humans should imitate the traits of Heaven: hierarchy, integrity, purpose, and propriety in relationships. In contrast, Zhuangzi's nature (Heaven) or its patterns (Dao) is devoid of all of these traits. To imitate the Dao, then, involves forgetting all of these traits.

Modeling on nature has an immediate impact on the use of language. Both the Confucians and Zhuangzi advocated using language that somehow corresponds to the Dao or to Heaven, but this meant entirely different things for each of them. For Confucians, language that corresponds to Heaven is language that promotes hierarchy and the other traits of nature. Proper language both reveals the speaker's correct standard and persuades other people to evaluate a situation the same way the speaker does. Choice of words combines facts and values. It describes and evaluates. To call a person "king" is not only to describe his position but also to affirm that he is acting in the manner in which an ideal king should act. Use of such a title also helps to maintain social hierarchies. In the case of Zhuangzi, the only use of language that corresponds to nature is language that the speaker does not take seriously. Language, with its hidden value standards embedded in words, does not correspond to any pattern in nature. Zhuangzi did not advocate remaining silent, but he did say that the way to imitate the Dao is not to be controlled by language or by those embedded customary standards.

Zhuangzi's Dao being purposeless, its changes unfold in an orderly way but not for the special benefit of humans or anything else. The Chinese expression wu-wei describes this trait. That expression originally meant "not to act for the sake of anything." Hence purposeless spontaneity is conduct that emulates the Dao. It is going in whatever direction natural changes lead a person. More precisely, this is conduct under the control of the individual's True Ruler, which is the Dao within each individual. To the degree that the individual behaves accordingly, the power (de) grows within him. The term wu-wei appears twice in the original Zhuangzi chapters, referring not directly to the Dao but to laid-back, free and easy roaming.[8]

Interestingly, the Zhuangzi and the Laozi do not have a monopoly on this idea of wu-wei. By at least the third century B.C. it was shared by diverse thinkers. One of its most common applications was to the ideal ruler who himself rests in the background, aloof from daily operations, while overseeing officials and institutions that handle administration. Such usage appears in the Confucian Xunzi text many times. Thus, before the end of the Warring States Period, Confucian spontaneity included both the idea of being so perfectly cultivated that one automatically does the morally right thing and also the ideal of a nonintrusive style by rulers.

Nature and Society. Zhuangzi was no advocate of the vegetative existence. Nonstriving meant not striving for wealth, status, power, long life, and the other goals that keep people galloping around. But adapting to objective conditions as they are is compatible with having a family and doing ordinary tasks. Zhuangzi himself was said to have had a family. He went along with the customary family obligations of his time, but he dramatically opened the door of legitimacy for a life contrasted with the ideal of official service, as was so strongly touted in the Confucian works. In the Analects of Confucius, Confucius's disciple Zi Lu says to a hermit's children concerning the importance of seeking public office: "How can it be right for a man to set aside the duty that binds minister to prince, or in his desire to maintain his own integrity, to subvert the Great Relationship?"[9]

A F T E R W O R D

Hermits do appear in the *Analects*, but they are escaping bad rulers and bad times. One infers that they would have liked to serve under other conditions. Zhuangzi stands for an alternative to official service or other high-status jobs, namely, accepting one's current situation, seeking solitude, or withdrawing from office. In our current text we read of a king who, on learning of the damage caused by the intellect, leaves the world and lives in a grass hut (p. 53). Confucius goes off to live in the forest and study the Dao, chastened about showing off his learning (p. 80). High positions may be necessary to society, but the wise person does not stick around those who occupy them (p. 70). They are dangerous (p. 124). There is a marvelous exchange in the "Autumn Floods" chapter of the *Zhuangzi*, written by followers of Zhuangzi whose ideas paralleled his own. Mindful that creatures honored at court (including sacrificial tortoises and cows) often lost their lives in the bargain, the author reports that Zhuangzi was once offered a high post in Chu. Zhuangzi replied to the officials sent to make the offer by reminding them of the sacred tortoise stored in the king's ancestral temple. Zhuangzi asked them if it would rather be alive in the mud or dead and honored. He matched their obvious reply with "Go away! I'll drag my tail in the mud."

Later Daoists, inspired by the door that Zhuangzi had opened to an alternative to the Confucian official service ideal, made much of refusal of or withdrawal from public service, whether the ruler was benevolent or not. Some prized the solitude of the recluse, but many Daoist hermits lived in groups. To be a recluse did not necessarily mean abandoning family; rather, it meant staying away from political involvement.

The Holistic Perspective. Our present text does not bring out one curious but important feature of Zhuangzi's writing that is suggested by the very idea that there is a preferred way to lead a life. As an opponent of pursuing goals derived from verbally definable standards, Zhuangzi had no equal. Yet he had his own goals, derived from treating the Dao as a unity that permeates or links together the many things.

One such goal was the achievement of a holistic perspective, the ability to regard something from many different angles. Obviously this ideal arose from the ability to "forget" the categories associated with particular schools of thought. Positively stated, it was the ability to soar freely through countless perspectives, perhaps mindful that each might have a piece of the truth. The following passage from one of the original *Zhuangzi* chapters uses the terms "this" and "that" to refer to different perspectives and their categories:

To show what each regards as right is wrong or to show that what each regards as wrong is right, there is no better way than to use the light (of Nature).

There is nothing that is not the "that" and there is nothing that is not the "this." Things do not know that they are the "that" of things; they only know what they themselves know. Therefore I say that the "that" is produced by the "this" and the "this" is also caused by the "that." This is the theory of mutual production. Nevertheless, when there is life there is death, and when there is death there is life. When there is possibility there is impossibility, and when there is impossibility, there is possibility. Because of the right, there is the wrong, and because of the wrong, there is the right.[10]

The standpoint of the Dao brings all of these arbitrarily acceptable and unacceptable positions into one, gathering the possible insight of each. The text goes on, "Therefore the sage does not proceed along these lines (of right and wrong, and so forth), but illuminates the matter with Nature. . . . The 'this' is also the 'that.' The 'that' is also the 'this.' "[11] Inspired by this idea, the follower of Zhuangzi who wrote the "Autumn Floods" chapter described Zhuangzi's current situation in this way: "To him there is no north or south—in utter freedom he dissolves himself in the four directions and drowns himself in the unfathomable. To him there is no east or west—he begins in the Dark Obscurity and returns to the Great Thoroughfare."[12]

The Great Thoroughfare is the Dao. The expression refers to the fact that as the timeless principle of change, it penetrates like a road through all the myriad things that undergo transformation from one physical form to another. Zhuangzi is free in the negative sense of being free from the constraints of a single perspective, the kind that enables the Mohist to understand only through Mohist categories and the Confucian through Confucian categories. He is free in the positive sense in that his mind can roam over most or all perspectives. This is one of the things that makes it possible for him to respond like a mirror to an objective situation in a way that completely reflects the objective situation rather than his own prejudices. Elsewhere in that same chapter, one of the characters remarks, "He who understands the Way is certain to have command of basic principles. He who has command of basic principles is certain to know how to deal with circumstances."[13]

The other positive value and goal that Zhuangzi derived from his insight about the unitary nature of the Dao was mystical. It was loss of awareness of self, to be replaced by awareness of participating in the Dao. Traditionally mystics in a variety of cultures have described at least two common claims in their writings. The first is that the proper perspective on the world is one that unifies the variety of experienced phenomena, and this perspective should inform one's attitude toward those things. Zhuangzi meets this criterion. A well-known passage in his chapter the "Discussion on Making All Things Equal" says "Heaven and earth were born at the same time I was, and the ten thousand things are one with me."[14] In addition to repeating this position, several of the other chapters speak of the perfected person as "having no self." He described such a condition as attainable through fasting—not the fasting that precedes religious sacrifice, but fasting the mind. This is emptying the mind of the control exercised by the categories through which one school of thought or perspective interprets the world.

Zhuangzi put into the mouth of Confucius's favorite disciple some words that express the idea of union with the Dao. This is the same disciple who told his master that he had been improving by forgetting the Confucian teachings of benevolence, righteousness, rites, and music. He continued: "I smash up my limbs and body, drive out perception and intellect, cast off form, do away with understanding, and make myself identical with the Great Thoroughfare. This is what I mean by sitting down and forgetting everything."[15] Our delightful cartoons convey this ideal quite nicely. One balloon (p. 54) reminds us that "Only the selfless person can live up to the standards of nature because your body is just one temporary form in nature's constantly changing process." We also find it in the verses on p. 53:

Don't see with your eyes,
Don't hear with your ears,

Don't think with your mind,
Embrace the primal one,
No knowledge, no self,
Go with nature,
Participate in nature, be one with nature,
And a long life will come naturally.

The other claim that mystics traditionally have made is that ordinary language is useless for describing mystical experiences. Zhuangzi's own position on the limitations and obstructions of language are by now well known to the reader. But it is interesting to note that he never discussed language and his own mystical experiences.

The topic of language and mysticism does raise the intriguing question of whether Zhuangzi's understanding of the ability of a person to understand the nature of the Dao involves verbal summation or intuitive insight. A reader could quite properly sum up the Dao from the traits that Zhuangzi explicitly attributes to it in language. In the "Discussion on Making All Things Equal" Zhuangzi wrote that "the Way has never known boundaries."[16] This is similar to the description of the Dao in the *Laozi* as an uncarved block. Individuated things occur objectively as transitory possessors of physical forms. Psychologically, individu-ation is the result of humans categorizing and classifying and tacking labels and evaluations onto those formed objects. The Dao is one. Humans are in part responsible for dividing it up into bounded parts, or for carving up the block. This is something they try to add onto reality. It is no part of reality itself. From this assertion that the Dao is unbounded, Zhuangzi or a reader could have deduced that we remain part of it, and that the individual should seek to become aware of this fact. The reasoning could continue that he should then treat as equal partners all other things that likewise are part of the Dao.

However, given his distaste for verbal argument, Zhuangzi would probably prefer the reader to treat his understanding of the Great Thoroughfare as an intuitive insight. That is why the pages so frequently refer to "using clarity" and why he says that the sage "illuminates the matter with Nature."[17] So, unlike the portrait of the human mind that some Westerners have derived from the Greeks via Descartes, the highest form of mental activity is not reasoning from rationally established axioms or innate truths, but it is simply intuitive insight. That insight into the Dao in turn manifests itself as adaptation to what nature brings our way. Modeling on nature is automatic.

Donald J. Munro
UNIVERSITY OF MICHIGAN

Notes

In interpreting the *Zhuangzi*, I am a transmitter more than an originator. I have learned enormously from the works of Angus C. Graham and Liu Xiaogan, and from my tutorials many years ago with Liu Yuyun. Liu Xiaogan's major work is *Zhuangzi zhexue ji qi yanbian* (*Zhuangzi's Philosophy and Its Evolutionary Change*) (Beijing:

Zhongguo shehui koxue chubanshe, 1987). In recent years I have also benefited from papers by Robert Eno and Margaret Suh. My understanding of Warring States Period history has been enriched by the chapter introductions and notes in John Knoblock, *Xunzi: A Translation and Study of the Complete Works*, vols. 1 and 2 (Stanford: Stanford University Press, 1988 and 1990).

1. *Laozi*, 51 in Wing-tsit Chan, *A Source Book in Chinese Philosophy* (Princeton, N.J.: Princeton University Press, 1973), p. 163.

2. Quoted in Fung Yu-lan, *A History of Chinese Philosophy*, trans. Derk Bodde (Princeton: Princeton University Press, 1952), 1: 198.

3. Ibid.

4. Burton Watson, trans., *The Complete Works of Chuang Tzu* (New York: Columbia University Press, 1968), p. 85.

5. Ibid., p. 97.

6. Angus C. Graham, *Chuang Tzu, The Inner Chapters* (London: Allen and Unwin, 1981), pp. 13–14.

7. Chan, *Source Book*, p. 38.

8. One is in chapter 1, which appears in this text on page 13, where it is rendered as "[to] rest" (meaning to do nothing), and the other appears in chapter 6 and can be found in ibid., p. 198. These were pointed out by Liu Xiaogan.

9. Arthur Waley, trans., *The Analects of Confucius* (New York: Random House, n.d.) 18.7.

10. Chan, *Source Book*, pp. 182–83.

11. Ibid.

12. Watson, *Chuang Tzu*, p. 187.

13. Ibid., p. 182.

14. Ibid., p. 43.

15. Ibid., p. 90. My understanding of the mysticism in Zhuangzi's writings was enriched by the writings of Dennis M. Ahern.

16. Ibid., p. 43.

17. Chan, *Source Book*, p. 183. Angus Graham alerted me to the significance of these passages.

ABOUT THE AUTHOR

Tsai Chih Chung is an immensely popular Taiwanese cartoonist. His cartoon characters entertain readers of Chinese all over the world, and his animation of his comic strip "Old Master Q" won a Golden Horse Award, the highest honor bestowed on filmmakers in Taiwan and Hong Kong.

Tsai began his career by crafting the adventures of characters such as the Drunken Swordsman, Fat Dragon, and Bald Supersleuth. Although his humorous characters and animated films have brought him great success, he has turned more recently to adapting and illustrating the works of ancient Chinese philosophy and literature. Thus far he has published nineteen volumes of such stories. Tsai's work is so popular in Taiwan that it accounts for three out of every four comic books sold there. The original edition of this book has gone through seventy-eight printings.

"Your life will be happier if you do not give yourself a rigid aim," Tsai says. "It's the process and not the result that counts. The swordsman should find happiness in learning to master the sword alone. For me, drawing cartoons is what I want to do, even if I have to survive on instant noodles."

Brian Bruya, a free-lance translator, first encountered Tsai Chih Chung's work while employed as a translator at The National Palace Museum in Taiwan.